# DEAR MUSES?

# By the same author:

# Dear Muses?

ESSAYS IN POETRY

\*

Simon West

PUNCHER & WATTMANN

First published in 2019
Published by Puncher and Wattmann
PO Box 441
Glebe NSW 2037
http://www.puncherandwattmann.com
puncherandwattmann@bigpond.com

ISBN 9781925780468

A catalogue record for this book is available from the National Library Australia.

Cover design by Miranda Douglas
Text design by Christine Bruderlin
Printed by Lightning Source International

This project has been assisted by the Australian Government through the Australia Council, its arts funding and advisory body.

# Contents

# Living Walls of Jet:
# Visiting the House of Poetry

*The purpose of poetry is to remind us*
*how difficult it is to remain just one person,*
*for our house is open, there are no keys in the doors,*
*and invisible guests come in and out at will.*
    (from 'Ars poetica?' Czesław Miłosz, trans. by the author
    and Lillian Vallee)

Let me start by asking you to imagine a house. Not your own house, but a dwelling you visit as a guest or stranger for the first time. Think about that moment of entering with all your senses on high alert. You take notice of the furnishings approvingly or disapprovingly, and you find yourself tempted to interpret the character of the occupants from the objects collected. But there is also something about being in an unfamiliar room that makes you feel slightly different yourself. You move around to get an idea of the place; you observe the way the windows frame the world outside; you start to feel at home or out of place, excited or dull; and all the time you're taking your bearings anew, as if this unfamiliar space stimulated you to experience yourself afresh.

In Italy, on entering a house as a guest it is customary to say *permesso?*. This expression might be translated as 'May I come in?', but it has become so habitual that it is often stated rather than inflected as a question. The word has become part of a ritual for acknowledging the moment of crossing a threshold.

I evoke such a moment because I see similarities with the way we encounter a poem. The word *stanza*, which we use to denote the paragraphs into which poems are divided, comes from the Italian word for *room*. John Donne was aware of this when he wrote 'The Canonization', the fourth stanza of which runs:

> Wee can dye by it, if not live by love,
> And if unfit for tombes or hearse
> Our legend bee, it will be fit for verse;
> And if no peece of Chronicle wee prove,
> We'll build in sonnets pretty roomes;
> As well a well wrought urne becomes
> The greatest ashes, as halfe-acre tombes,
> And by these hymnes, all shall approve
> Us *Canoniz'd* for Love.

'We'll build in sonnets pretty roomes' is characteristic of Donne's wit and playfulness. It could have served Samuel Johnson an example of the Metaphysical's intellectual showiness. But I like to think there is something about Donne's pun across languages that resonates with deeper truths. I want to explore how a poem *is* a room, one in which words establish a space wherein they harmonize with each other in fresh ways, and in which we as readers come to take our bearings.

We often talk of the structural integrity of a poem to refer to metre and verbal echoes such as rhyme and alliteration. They seem to create a verbal architecture. This architectural analogy is not limited to traditional verse, for it can narrow in to the level of syntax and word, or extend out to the level of theme. In using architectural images, I do not want to suggest that words are locked in place, riveted like traves in a wall. Language is a dynamic system, and we delight in the infinite potential for creating connections between words. Coleridge once described this (using a neologism of Donne's, incidentally) as the 'inter-inanimation of words'. Like the house of language which, for Heidegger, became a metaphor for our active dwelling in the world, the rooms of poetry are fluid spaces of encounter.

Often the most important of these encounters is with language itself. Unlike its cousin, prose, poetry can't rely on those two cornerstones of dynamism: plot and character. It has a different sort of energy, one which lies in language itself. Language is the protagonist of poetry. In a poem every word is a proper noun. Seamus Heaney saw language as a current that sweeps us up. The poem's impetus may start in personal experience, but it moves beyond that quickly, so that 'sound and meaning rise like a tide out of language to carry individual utterance away upon a current stronger and deeper than the individual could have anticipated'.

It is the stanza of poetry that allows language to take on the role of heroine. In the successful poem readers enter to take stock of themselves, just as a tourist might enter a church or a temple simply to take a deep breath. Words need these refuges. Languages get battered and dematerialized through daily use. The most common words can appear threadbare. A poem aims to create the context in which they can resonate more richly. It's like going to a wedding: the sense of occasion is such that when the speakers stand to evoke words that elsewhere would sound like clichés, they rediscover an authenticity that can move the audience to tears.

That community coming together to celebrate a wedding is a timely qualifier of what I have said so far. The focus on language is only part of poetry's remit. I don't want to suggest the poem is removed from reality, like a bunker for the isolated individual. Donne talks of this. The Copernican Revolution seems to have led to a cultural crisis not dissimilar to our own, at least as the 'Anatomy of the World' describes:

> 'Tis all in pieces, all coherence gone;
> All just supply, and all Relation:
> Prince, Subject, Father, Sonne are things forgot,
> For every man alone thinks he hath got
> To be a Phoenix, and that there can be
> None of that kinde, of which he is, but hee.

The phoenix is a wonderful figure of comparison for this crisis. It is a symbol of instability because it must consume and reinvent itself in continuation. But it also lives in isolation — only a single phoenix was thought to exist at any one time.

So it is to the image of the open house, the house as conviviality, coming together, the moment of voicing 'permesso!' that I would like to return. The room, after all, returns in another poem by Donne, 'The Good Morrow'. Here, like man, the room is a microcosm and mirror of the world at large as it makes 'one little room an everywhere'.

> And now good morrow to our waking soules,
> Which watch not one another out of feare;

For love, all love of other sights controules,
And makes one little roome, an everywhere.
Let sea-discoverers to new worlds have gone,
Let Maps to others, worlds on worlds have shown,
Let us possesse one world, each hath one, and is one.

Why should it be love that turns a room into an everywhere, and two lovers into one perfect unity? For Donne, in his youth, love was thickly infused with Platonism, love of a type that struggled to find its feet in modernity. But once again we should be careful to dismiss it. Donne's words sink their foundations into a truer ground, and this allows them to resonate further down the ages. This love between two people does not obliterate everywhere else. It transforms the room into a microcosm of community and the world at large. Could we not argue that poetry does something similar in its own rooms? Since poetry is made from the stuff of language, and words are products of human society, the poem embodies the spirit not only of communication, but of community.

Donne's poetry is charged with such a spirit. One final image evokes this well. In 'The Flea' that most intimate of insects symbolises the communion of the lovers by mingling their blood:

This flea is you and I, and this
Our marriage bed, and marriage temple is;
Though parents grudge, and you, w'are met,
And cloistered in these living walls of Jet.

The flea *is* you and I. Donne suggests we must seek to draw connections between ourselves and others, and between ourselves and the world at large, and thereby hope to understand a little more clearly the state of reality in which we exist. It is in poetry's living walls of jet that we begin to do this.

## Works Cited

John Donne, *The Elegies and Songs and Sonnets*, edited by Helen Gardner, Oxford University Press, 1965.

John Donne, *The Divine Poems*, edited by Helen Gardner, Second Ed., Oxford University Press, 1978.

Seamus Heaney, *Finders Keepers, Selected Prose*, Faber and Faber, 2002.

Czesław Miłosz, *New and Collected Poems*, Ecco, 2001.

# Dear Muses? John Forbes and a Classical Heritage in Contemporary Australian Poetry

Does it make sense to invoke the Muses in Australia today? If you come across a reference to Calliope or her sisters in poetry of the last one hundred years it is likely to be ironic. Few of us believe our poems will be better for praying to a committee of stola-clad ladies sitting on a mountain in Greece. It is easy to parody this representation, and in doing so, to mark our distance from the world of Parnassus. Inspiration now takes other forms.

But is there a different way in which we can still invoke the Muses? When Dante summons these pagans in his Christian epic their presence cannot be fully explained through literary convention, or irony, or a belief in pantheism. They have become a mouthpiece for the poet to acknowledge the continuing importance of a cultural heritage that radiates out from the Classical world and into the present day. In addressing the Muses we talk to that inheritance. We also take on the role of custodians, with a responsibility both to preserve it and to be aware of the ways we appropriate and transform it creatively.

\*

In the introduction to their anthology *Contemporary Australian Poetry*, the editors identify an underlying incredulity in the Australian psyche, a reluctance to believe wholeheartedly in affirmations of truth and belief. They go on to say, 'we do not have the traditions, found in some European or Asian nations, which can operate as substitutes for belief', but rather, we are a sort of natural postmodern country, 'one that arrived at the groundlessness of postmodernism through cultural and geographic circumstances'. I'm not so sure. I think we have maintained strong ties to a range of traditions, and our poets have been instrumental in keeping them alive.

In this essay I want to argue for the continuing importance of a classical heritage and its later European manifestations in the evolving creation of an Australian poetic culture. Sometimes we present those traditions as a burden or even an obstacle. To show deference to them — with their deities and dainty tropes — has been thought a betrayal of the unique qualities of our here and now, and a perpetuation of our colonial yoke. But in shaking off that yoke we need to be careful not to collapse the distinction between the British Empire and the Roman, between the Victorians and Virgil. I'm interested in poets who are engaged in a struggle with the past and seek to transform it into new forms of art. The tactics employed are ecumenical rather than insular. They seek to reanimate rather than ridicule the Muses.

I want to take that figure of the Muse, together with her cousin the Sibyl, as symbols of a Classical tradition and ask what place they may still have in contemporary Australian poetry. Is it possible to evoke them today without constraining ourselves within markers of disbelief? Can we sign a poem that takes up

Aphrodite today 'yours sincerely'? I will start and finish with a brief discussion of two poems of my own, but the core of the essay considers John Forbes. I don't want to suggest the superiority of my work by bookending Forbes in this way. This essay began as an attempt at self-reflection. As I was writing, it seemed appropriate to turn, as a point of contrast, to one of our best poets to have engaged with these issues in ways I had imagined to be different to my own.

*

In 'Volatiles', a poem I published in *The Yellow Gum's Conversion*, there is a reference to a Sibyl. The poem begins:

> Strange for the season, but there it was,
> a cold wind from the south. Dead or insect-
> ravaged leaves were shaken off rivergums
> and whirled hard across a tract where the Goulburn
> opened the bush like a furrow. It pulled me up,
> as if a Sibyl's scattered forecasts
> were there for the grabbing.
> Each had turned to a hovering moment,
> a way back to reckon the day's alloy,
> odd as a bowerbird's hoard: bright trinket-words,
> gut-wrenches, regrets. . . .

Following publication I received a comment, given half in jest, to the effect that my classical reference was out of place in Australia today. The Sibyls were oracles said once to have inhabited holy sites in Greece and Italy such as Delphi and Cumae. Since the time of Virgil and his contemporaries they have also inhabited and loomed large in Western literature. It was at Cumae that the Sibyl famously wrote the answer to questions on a leaf and then summoned a wind to scatter the leaves, making the answer the supplicant required so close at hand and yet impossible to obtain. Dante reimagined the Sibyl of Cumae in the final canto of the *Commedia*, at the point when he is searching for similes to describe how difficult it is to formulate and hold onto the vision he has just witnessed:

*così la neve al sol si disigilla*
*così al vento ne le foglie levi*
*si perdea la sentenza di Sibilla.*

just as snow melts in the sun,
just as the oracles the Sibyl wrote on leaves
were scattered by the wind.
[Paradiso 33, 61–63]

I liked the idea of imagining a Sibyl in a landscape which was typical of the Goulburn Valley in north-central Victoria. It seemed to enrich the long tradition of evoking such classical figures in Western poetry by imagining them in a radically new context, but it also allowed me to affirm these places, the floodplains of river red gums along the Broken and Goulburn rivers, places I had long thought I needed to escape from, as worthy of poetry.

That juxtaposition pleased me because it embodied the uneasy way my allegiances lie with my language as much as they do with the places in which I dwell. In the case of English, the languages and stories of the Greeks and the Latins underpin a portion of our cultural heritage. It seemed right to continue to explore those stories and etymologies, even in the antipodes, however antediluvian they might appear. Wasn't this reimagining of a pagan figure in a Christian context, for example, what Dante had done in the culminating final canto of his epic, right at the point in which he is struggling to find a way to retell his vision of God? Milton does something similar at the opening of Book 7 of *Paradise Lost*:

> *Descend from Heav'n, Urania, by that name*
> *If rightly thou art call'd whose voice divine*
> *Following, above th' Olympain Hill I soare,*
> *Above the flight of Pegasean wing.*
> *The meaning, not the Name I call: for thou . . .*
> *Nor of the Muses nine, nor on the top*
> *Of old Olympus dwell'st, but heav'nly-borne*
> *Before the Hills appeerd, or Fountain flowd,*
> *Thou with Eternal Wisdom didst converse.*

It wasn't subservience to a tradition, then, but an attempt to keep the two, the old and the new, in a working and vital relationship. I wanted to find a way to transform that inheritance into a work of art that might be faithful to our own age, while paying homage to our ancestors.

Perhaps what I had not adequately done was to signal a distrust of those traditions in the poem itself. One method often employed to signal distrust of received ideas or mythologies is the use of irony. Indeed what my local critic specifically found missing in 'Volatiles' was an ironic stance. Irony would allow my poem to signal its awareness of the complex tradition of invoking a sibyl and its limitations as myth, but at the same time assert its own independence and autochthonous interests. Irony might be a way of distinguishing my own aestheticising of the landscape from that of a nineteenth-century poet like Barron Field, who wrote in 'Kangaroo':

Kangaroo, Kangaroo!
Thou Spirit of Australia,

That redeems from utter failure,
From perfect desolation,
And warrants the creation
Of this fifth part of the Earth,
Which would seem an after-birth,
Not conceiv'd in the Beginning
(For GOD bless'd His work at first,
And saw that it was good),
But emerg'd at the first sinning,
When the ground was therefore curst; —
And hence this barren wood!

Here, of course, the retelling of the Genesis myth to incorporate 'this fifth part of the Earth' evokes biblical rather than classical traditions in its dismissive vision of the colonists' new environment. However, the epigraph to this poem, 'mixtumque genus, prolesque biformis', comes from a description of the Minotaur in Book VI of the *Aeneid*. In Field's poem there is a clear subservience to the 'imported' tradition and its values to which the new landscape fails to adhere. That failure, that lack of known tropes, would allow the landscape to be cleared and settled imaginatively in such poems, just as it was physically by the axe and bullock team.

There is in such fawning to tradition as model, and in such little regard for the actuality of the new context in which Field finds himself, a pretension and a disjunct which I do not look kindly on. I liked to imagine my own piece had found a better balance, in which old and new were in dialogue. I didn't feel the need to place the sibyl in quotation marks, because the reference was not a pretension of knowledge of a classical tradition that somehow validated the poem's colonisation and naming of the Goulburn river. Rather, it threw them together on equal footing.

Just as I felt the two ideas vied equally for attention in myself — the landscape which I had trod since birth, and the language I had uttered in time to that walking. Furthermore, I felt the colloquial opening, 'Strange for the season', together with words like 'reckon', and phrases like 'odd as a bowerbird' and 'gut-wrenches', all obviated in their own small way any pretensions to self-importance and deference to the past which might be associated with the evocation of a sibyl.

The editors of *Contemporary Australian Poetry* also identify the way distrust often manifests locally in the colloquial tenor of Australian speech. 'The colloquial is, among other things, the speech of the abrasive testing of one's peers, of the persistent challenge to unfounded statements'. The colloquial is a powerful challenge to the pretensions of importance when they manifest in language. The politician's weasel words, the theorist's abstractions, the poet's tired rhetoric and tropes are all cut down to size by colloquial speech. Some of our best poets, Les Murray foremost among them, have been masters of this use of language. At times the colloquial has been tied to a nationalist agenda. But the link is not set in stone. The colloquial is plain speech, and hence, parochial in the good sense of that word. It exists everywhere, with its own personality, in each family or group where verbal communication is vibrant and essential to life.

## Dwelling on Nature's Nothing

The classical Greek word from which our own term irony derives is εἰρωνεία. In Greek comedy the Eiron was the underdog who regularly triumphed over the boastful poser, the Alazon, thanks to his wit. If the editors of *Contemporary Australian Poetry* are correct, then perhaps Eiron could be adopted as a typically Australian character, for irony is an expression of the speaker's reluctance to believe. For Socrates the word irony was closely associated with the idea of dissimulation affected to provoke or confound an antagonist. Socrates would profess to know nothing, but then proceeded to show that his adversary knew even less. In the *Nicomachean Ethics* Aristotle placed εἰρωνεία at one pole whose opposite was false pretension. Here εἰρωνεία seems to have been closer in meaning to what we would term 'understatement'. Roger Crisp in his translation of the *Nicomachean Ethics* uses the term 'self deprecation', which makes sense in that context, since Aristotle is discussing individual virtues. But it can be useful to extend Aristotle's dichotomy and consider irony as a powerful corrective against pretensions of knowledge and self-importance, whether it be directed at ourselves or at others.

We still need irony today. It is difficult, however, to generalize about irony since it has more shades of colour than a paint shop, and is harder to pin down than tone of voice. It's worth recalling the more extreme end of Socratic irony, one which has been to the fore in the last century or two and remains with us today. This is where irony is employed not as a corrective, but as an end in itself, as an expression of negativity. At this point it is hard to distinguish irony from hopelessness. John Donne captured something of this in 'A Litany' when he tells us to take care:

> that wit born apt high good to doe,
> by dwelling lazily
> on Nature's nothing, be not nothing too.

Wit is a close relative of irony. In both we find quick intelligence gets to the heart of things, cutting through the bombast to reveal a barer but truer vision. Originally wit meant mental capacity, knowledge, understanding. Donne is enunciating an important warning, however. Wit has the capacity to do great good, to challenge unfounded pretensions and false sincerities, but it needs to be kept in check.

The Italian word for wit is *ingegno*, which can also cover the idea of genius. For Dante, wit is a gift from God and must be used wisely to help bring man closer to the divine. In Dante's portrait of Ulysses, that Greek hero has the gift of genius and a tongue of flame that can dance with eloquence and stir up passions in a crowd. He also has a passion to understand the world in all its facets. He is driven by a desire for knowledge. And yet for Dante there was something flawed in Ulysses' character. We encounter it when wit and irony exceed their remit as a tool to dismantle the pretensions of an adversary. Instead they destroy all common ground, even that of language. We might call it irony as *modus vivendi*, as expression of nihilism.

## 'O Palpitations, go away!'

At first glance John Forbes would seem to be a poet who throws off the past in order to write a poetry that is faithful to the present. In her Foreword to Forbes' *Collected Poems*, Gig Ryan celebrates the 'faultlessly contemporary and anti-nostalgic' voice of Forbes. *Collected Poems* offers a number of references to the past in just this light. Take, for example, 'the way to beat inflation is to live in the past', and 'I want to believe the beautiful lies / the past spreads out like a feast'. In each case Forbes collapses an important distinction between living in and relating to the past. 'Why not forget everything / Patrick White ever wrote?' he provokes in 'Sydney'. This is a poetry that beautifully captures the spirit of scepticism and self-confidence of a group of poets who found their voice in the seventies. As he writes in the opening of 'Rocket to Rome', which is subtitled 'Homage to the Ramones':

Read about the Goliard Poets
so long dead & so like you —

*sile philomela pro tempore*
*surge cantilena de pectore*

and think how little you deserve
the kisses of the Muse you serve,

play rock'n'roll for hours
until the neighbours cower . . .

The Goliard poets are fitting precursors to Forbes with that motto 'keep quiet, nightingale, and let me sing!' The nightingale might easily stand in for tradition. Throw it off in favour of self-expression and rock'n'roll. This is poetry that has learnt from Frank O'Hara to go on its nerve.

And yet Forbes is often a more complex poet than he at first appears. 'Rocket to Rome' is typical in its continual interrogation of what sort of heritage we might expect from Rome. The poem seeks alternative forebears in the Goliards and Joey Ramone, but it doesn't dismiss the past outright. Similarly, that line about forgetting Patrick White in the poem 'Sydney' is followed by a quote from Christopher Brennan, 'My days of azure have forgotten me'. Sampled for its incongruousness? Perhaps. But perhaps not, given that the narrator (addressing himself in the second person singular) then talks of '. . . cerulean music / coming out of your head'. It's absurd and slightly tongue-in-cheek — but only slightly. Brennan and White with their status in the canon persist to challenge Forbes. The end of the poem makes this very clear, for it picks up the well-worn trope that says literature can outlast death:

others have armchairs
& opinions about things

but you sing a song like
the clinking of schooners

the city's still hearing
when they're dead & gone

White, Brennan, and Forbes himself all seem to have booked their places in a common pantheon. Forbes satirizes the tradition, but in doing so he reveals his own investment in it. He is struggling against rather than ignoring his forerunners.

There is a restless and unceasing need to compare the here and now in Australia with the elsewhere and former in Forbes, from early on in pieces like 'Four Heads & how to do them', to a poem like 'Anzac Day'. In this last piece, while other nations earnestly and self-deludingly assigned significance to sacrifice for one's country, Australian soldiers were different: 'unamused, unimpressed / they went over the top like men clocking on'. Forbes might be the most patriotic poet we have produced, and the one who expresses the most confidence in being Australian. In these comparisons he is irreverent rather than deferential as he challenges Europe and its traditions to live up to the hype. Take for example, 'Admonition', quoted whole:

Be still, my beating heart, & you, body
Don't go banging into that tree—
The one the girl turned into, back
When the gods were like they are
In the Collected Poems of A.D. Hope.
& arms stop waving and legs don't dance
As if an invisible band was playing

A Fitzroy version of 'Picture This'.
Consider instead this cool Melbourne
Morning & the iconic self it suggests;
The laundromat, the review you haven't
Written yet, or choosing 5 dead certs
For an all-up bet (& when they win
You blow the lot on bills and rent!)
That's Grace enough this mild autumn day, so
Like I say, Oh palpitations, go away!

'When the gods were like they are / in the Collected Poems of A. D. Hope', he writes with considerable sarcasm. The bluntness of the address, and the playful questioning of the disjunct between imported tradition and local environment, seem typically Australian in character, and contrast with the patrician tone of much of Hope's poetry.

In 'Admonition' the narrator tries to ignore what the body is saying. He tries to convince himself of the absurdity of continuing to make use of a tradition of love poetry with its tropes of heart palpitations, the body-mind disjunct, and metamorphosis. After all, these tropes are perpetuated out of laziness rather than suitability to Melbourne in the 1990s. And yet there is something futile in that final imperative to go away. The beauty of the poem lies in the fact that the palpitations won't leave, and won't be convinced by argument, because they are as irrational as love itself. The narrator is compelled to undergo the litany of clichés associated with unrequited love, and the poet is compelled to write about them.

It is surprising just how many of Forbes' poems are unrequited love poems. Like the narrator of 'Admonition', many poems mock not so much the traditional tropes associated with love, but rather the poet's inability to get beyond them:

Your feelings return
like duped insurgents, clogging
the streets with their tears.

This is from 'Holy Week'. There is also this from 'The Harbour Bride':

Her barge is bedecked
with bales of yellow $50 notes
& you can't believe it
as she disappears towards Vaucluse —
your suntanned Aphrodite,
waving
almost reluctantly,
goodbye to you

In 'Love Poem' the Iraq war becomes an objective correlative for the poet's morose love-sickness. The poem is saved from bathos by the self irony of lines like, 'as I curl up with the war / in lieu of you'. But if the irony creates some distance from the initial sentiment, we're talking millimetres rather than miles. In 'Rocket to Rome' he had written:

and think how little you deserve
the kisses of the Muse you serve.

Ultimately, Forbes is forced to admit that, despite his love for the Ramones, despite the urge to throw off the past, he too has been faithful to the Muse.

Finally, I turn to 'On Tiepolo's Banquet of Cleopatra', a poem which uses the eighteenth-century Venetian painting housed in the National Gallery of Victoria as a mirror for looking at our own world. Here is the first half of the poem:

Any frayed waiting room copy of *Who*
could catch this scene: flash Euro-
trash surveys a sulky round faced
überBabe who's got the lot — what else
could this painting mean, except that
superstars can will their luck, or
just how little raw envy's hidden by
contempt, so words like 'Wow! Great
Tits!' or 'Comic Opera Wop' sum up
the observer, not Anthony and Cleopatra,
attached to pets & entourages — our
contemporaries minus coke and sunglasses.

I find the narrative voice difficult to interpret in this poem. I
am struck by that phrase, 'what else could this painting mean'. I
can't help hearing it as a reductive assertion, rather than a prof-
fered challenge to the reader, as if the poem might boil down
to the thought, 'Who needs Tiepolo, or the classical heroes he
represents in his paintings, when we have the same thing in contemporary Australian culture? I sense that same bravura attitude
in the use of the word 'minus' in the last line. But then the poem
turns to address the reader directly. Or is it Forbes who inter-
rogates himself? He asks, is our contempt for Tiepolo's scene,
which expresses itself in the vulgar colloquialisms, really a ploy
to conceal our envy? Envy of what? Of the lavish lifestyle of
ephemeral celebrities, sure, but also the longevity and lavishness
of our European heritage. It is this durability of Antony and
Cleopatra — the fact that painters and writers have built up
accretions of meaning around their names for 2000 years —
that distinguishes them from our contemporaries. In this regard
they are minus nothing, and harder to dimiss than the latest
gossip magazine.

## Aletheia

In *A Defence of Ardor*, the Polish poet Adam Zagajewski describes how in our world, contrary to the classical world, irony has come to express a disillusionment 'with the collapse of utopian expectations, an ideological crisis provoked by the erosion and discrediting of those visions that hoped to replace the traditional metaphysics of religious faith with eschatological political theories'. Zagajewski suggests we don't need to abandon irony, but rather to recognise that it is not a primary building block of art. 'Only ardor is a primary building block in our literary constructions. Irony is, of course, indispensable, but it comes later, . . . it is more like the windows and doors without which our buildings would be solid monuments, not habitable spaces.' Zagajewski is coy about what exactly ardour looks like. But we might imagine that in the case of the poet, it will include a love of language, and the effort to speak sincerely through such a medium. This in turn requires a cherishing of the stories and etymologies that each word stores within itself like a tabernacle.

Another Polish writer, Czesław Miłosz, finds in his poetry a balance between the constructive, ecstatic, positive platonic desires in us which we might associate with Zagajewski's ardour, and the down-to-earth scepticism of our current culture. He frequently adopts irony, but as with Forbes' love poems, it is most often directed at himself, and counterbalanced by what he calls 'a passionate search for the real'. Miłosz' poetry is both affirmation and negation; exuberant celebration of the world and self critical mockery of one's own desires. Take for example the poem 'Magpiety':

The same and not quite the same, I walked through oak forests
Amazed that my Muse, Mnemosyne,

Has in no way diminished my amazement.
A magpie was screeching and I said: Magpiety?
What is magpiety? I shall never achieve
A magpie heart, a hairy nostril over the beak, a flight
That always renews just when coming down,
And so I shall never comprehend magpiety.
If however magpiety does not exist
My nature does not exist either.
Who would have guessed that, centuries later,
I would invent the question of universals?
[trans. Czesław Miłosz and Peter Dale Scott]

In Aristotle's use of the term εἰρωνεία in the *Nichomachean Ethics* there was a middle point or golden mean between *alazoneia* (boastfulness) and *eironeia*. We swing between a pretence of knowledge spurred on by earnestness and self-importance; and at the other extreme, the despair of hopelessness and doubt which push us to an attitude of irony and sarcasm. But at the midpoint, difficult to hold, like trying to walk a tightrope above an abyss, Aristotle placed *aletheia*, truthfulness, sincerity. I like this idea because it reminds us that irony is an important tool to keep the ego from over-inflating, while recognising that there's something harder to seek out as well.

In a recent poem I took up some of these ideas. It is called 'A Twenty-First-Century Poet Timidly Addresses the Muse'.

Dear Muse, I know a man who has vowed to wink
whenever he invokes you. His poems gauge
the tightness of the lips that make a smile
hover between a sneer and dispassionate play.
Some have played the role of Socrates
so well their wit has hardened into zeal.
Although they have demeaned their enemies

the price is our shared vision of what's real.
I don't know if you wear a swimming costume,
flaunting your features and eternal youth,
or, dressed in a stola, you control the tribune,
or yearn like the Sibyl in her cave for death.
Rather I think of world-old anima mundi,
and know where I find my words in unison
it was miracle not acumen of mine
that took the lead, some timely intuition
that cuts across the nihilistic bars
we hold before the world. I think of how
you sanction song that calls the moon and stars.
Stand by me, Muse. Without you we would howl.

Way back in Imperial Rome, Horace happily invokes a pantheon of gods he didn't seem to believe in. The only explanation I can imagine is this was a way to acknowledge the Greek tradition to which Horace felt beholden. Like the poets of recent generations in Australia, Horace and his contemporaries must have been keenly aware of the disjunct between imported tradition and local environment. Yet this 'sucking at the dugs of Greece', as Yeats described it, this faith in tradition, came to be considered something Latin authors were eager to maintain and adapt to their own cultural environment.

How do we relate to the complexities of our literary tradition? I have the feeling that Dante's call to the Muses is more urgent in a place like contemporary Australia. Such is our distance from Europe and the living signs of its past, that we can more easily represent its various manifestations, including those Muses, as a caricature that highlights our differences better than it draws out affinities. If that assertion of contrast has been a strength of our poetic culture, it can also be a limit in moments when our confidence in the uniqueness of the Australian land-scape, for example, is undercut by awareness of environmental degradation; of when the search for an autochthonous poetry is stymied by colonial guilt. We are like the Romans looking to the Greeks, yet proudly ourselves, and riddled with doubt due to our colonial predicament.

Auden once wrote that, 'art is our chief means of breaking bread with the dead, and without communion with the dead a fully human life is impossible'. I like that image. It evokes the idea of sharing and mutual respect, of fellowship. It also recalls that the gift of language has been passed down to us from our forebears to be cared for in a relationship of custodianship. It is not a tool to use and abuse. It hints at the attempt to speak with Aristotle's truthfulness, while being aware of the difficulty of so doing.

The Muses are a good example of this bread-breaking because as we evoke them they become our interlocutors. They put us in contact with a river of poetry that has flowed for thousands of years. Of course they come with cultural baggage. Historically the Muses have been gendered as female, symbols of irrational poetic power to be harnessed and controlled by the male poet. We should be wary of these dynamics. But as creative writers we have the choice between dismissal on the one hand, and recu-peration and adaptation on the other. To my mind something vital and necessary persisted in the Muse. It did not have to be a worn-out trope, redolent of sexual dichotomies Germaine Greer takes aim at in her book *Slip-Shod Sibyls*. I liked to think the Muse might continue as an embodiment of the idea that poetry does not exist in a vacuum, and does not arise exclusively from the genius or angst of the individual. Much of the grind of exis-tence works against poetry. In those brief moments when we find an openness to the world, and the stars and our disparate thoughts align, a poem may germinate. When it does its arrival is something of a miracle, Muse-given.

I mentioned a river of poetry in the previous paragraph, and perhaps it requires further elucidation. There has long been a connection between rivers and poetry. Horace in Ode IV 2 famously described Pindar as a river in flood, rushing down a mountainside:

*monte decurrens velut amnis, imbres*
*quem super notas aluere ripas,*
*fervet immensusque ruit profundo*
*Pindarus ore.*

like a river rushing down a mountainside, swollen by rains above its normal banks, Pindar boils and surges immeasurably on with his deep booming voice [trans. Niall Rudd].

Dante takes up the image to describe Virgil when they first meet in the opening canto of his *Commedia*. However, he transforms the river into something more than a symbol of impetuous verbal power. Virgil embodies a spiritual and linguistic fecundity that has nourished future readers and writers:

*Or se' tu quel Virgilio e quella fonte*
*che spandi di parlar sì largo fiume?*

So are you Virgil, that source of speech
that grows into a wide river?

Knowledge as a stream works well because it maintains the fluid nature of our understanding. It recalls another image with which I would like to end — that of the Greek meander pattern. The meander is a continuous line symbolising unity and infinity. Unlike our use of the verb meander, it does not suggest wandering aimlessly. It has forward impetus, and yet that impetus is checked by a curving backwards, like a series of waves. In this way our desire to move forwards is balanced and enriched by keeping one eye on the past.

## Works Cited

Aristotle, *Nicomachean Ethics*, trans. and ed. Roger Crisp, Cambridge University Press, 2000.

W. H. Auden, ' *Prose Volume VI 1969–1973*, ed. Edward Mendelson, Princeton University Press, 2015.

John Donne, *The Divine Poems*, ed. Helen Gardner, 2nd ed., Oxford University Press, 1978.

John Forbes, *Collected Poems, 1970–1998*, Foreword by Gig Ryan, Brandl & Schlesinger, 2001.

Germaine Greer, *Slip-Shod Sibyls*, Penguin, 1996.

Horace, *Odes*, ed. and trans. Niall Rudd, Harvard University Press, 2004.

Rex Ingamells, *Conditional Culture*, F. W. Preece,1938.

Martin Langford, Judith Beveridge, Judy Johnson and David Musgrave (eds.), *Contemporary Australian Poetry*, Puncher & Wattmann, 2016.

Czesław Miłosz, *New and Collected Poems*, 1931–2001, Ecco, 2001.

John Milton, *The Poetical Works of John Milton*, ed. Helen Darbishire, Oxford University Press, 1958.

Simon West, *The Yellow Gum's Conversion*, Puncher & Wattmann, 2011.

Adam Zagajewski, *A Defence of Ardor*, trans. from Polish by Clare Cavanagh, Farrar, Straus and Giroux, 2004.

# Great Poem Hoax:
# On Gwen Harwood

In August 1961, the Melbourne newspaper *Truth* ran the headline GREAT POEM HOAX: HOUSEWIFE FOOLS THE EXPERTS WITH HER NAUGHTY SONNETS. The page three article began:

> A Tasmanian poet-housewife has become the centre of a literary storm because of two sonnets she sent to a magazine as a hoax. The sonnets concealed a message — and a rude word — in words from the first letter of each line. The poet is Mrs Gwen Harwood, of Hobart, wife of a University Tasmania lecturer . . . The first sonnet said 'So long, Bulletin'. The second gave an earthy and uncomplimentary opinion of all editors.

A similar piece in the *Daily Telegraph* stated:

> The mother of four schoolchildren said she does not write poetry as a hobby, and added 'I am a serious poet'.

Housewife or serious poet? What was Harwood? The acrostic in question, with its opening 'So Long, Bulletin', suggests a valedictory gibe after a rich and varied literary career. The reality was that Gwen Harwood, aged 41, had not yet published a volume of poetry. She had attracted the attention of James McAuley and A. D. Hope with a handful of poems published in the *Bulletin* and *Meanjin*, but for most Australians, including those whose news came from sources other than *Truth* or the *Daily Telegraph*, her name was a mystery. The fracas that ensued threw her into the spotlight. While she would go on to publish six major collections, and to hold a place among the best Australian writers of her generation (for Peter Porter she was 'the outstanding Australian poet of the twentieth century'), this early incident would continue to mark her career.

Fifty years later the 'So Long, Bulletin' hoax may appear a storm in a teacup, sadly indicative of the period's provincialism and prudishness. At the time, however, it became rather nasty. The *Bulletin* issue was recalled, and there were angry responses in the literary and wider press. There were rumours of legal repercussions. After all, Harwood was guilty of sneaking into print the same word which had been the focus of charges of obscenity against *Lady Chatterley's Lover* when the unexpurgated edition was released in 1960. Though, as she wrote to her lifetime confidant Tony Riddell:

> It would be interesting to see the lawyers prove that the sonnets contained obscene material; I don't suppose British law provides for vertical readings of poetry. If only you were here to laugh about this, but I do feel pretty much on my own and pretty much abandoned by the poets; nobody has written to thank me for drawing attention to the need for editorial competence.

In the tradition of Ern Malley, the two sonnets in question, 'Eloisa to Abelard' and 'Abelard to Eloïsa', were written to test the prowess of editors. Harwood maintained they had a limited value as poetry, and never republished them. They appeared under the pseudonym of Walter Lehmann. Harwood had begun to experiment with pseudonyms in 1959, using the addresses of friends and of her mother to elaborate the ruse. The first was W. W. Hagendoor (an anagram of her own name), whose work was never published. Other names followed, each with a life story and character traits: Walter Lehmann and Francis Geyer (both published repeatedly in the *Bulletin* until discovered), and then Miriam Stone. Harwood would eventually include some of their poems in her first two collections under her own name. However, poems first published under a later pseudonym, Timothy Kline, were not republished by Harwood. More recently, two poems published under the name of Alan Carvosso have surfaced.

A number of explanations have been given for the pseudonyms and their importance in Harwood's work. One of the primary reasons was the desire to test the waters of the Australian literary scene, and fathom that deepest of mysteries, the judgement of editors. It is worth remembering that the pseudonyms pertain to the period before she established herself as a poet. Her letters, which document so beautifully her struggles to make a name for herself, reveal a degree of youthful naivety about the world of letters. In 1960, she wrote to Tony Riddell:

> No wonder I'm becoming a raving paranoiac. Enclosed is a copy of the innocuous 'All Souls'. WHY WHY WHY does McA[uley] reject the intricate fusion of 'Sunday' and take this undistinguished piece? It is beyond my mental powers to follow an Editorial train of thought of this kind.

The idealist in Harwood seems to be crying out, 'how dare our literary elders be so wayward in their judgement, and so far from perfect'. What factors lay behind the acceptance or rejection of a poem? Would she have more chance at publication if she wrote as a man (aside from Miriam, all her pseudonyms were male), or as a north-European refugee, or if the postmark on the letters came from some godforsaken place like Orange? If she had recalled Doctor Johnson's remark that while an author is yet living we estimate his powers by his worst performance, and when he is dead we rate them by his best, her outrage may have turned earlier into cynicism, and Walter Lehmann might never have been born. As it was, Lehmann's acrostics would show up editors who were 'probably reading sideways as usual'.

If outrage was a strong motivation, there were other reasons for the masks. Certainly they reveal a youthful desire to experiment, and an anxiety about finding a voice that is recognisable. In 1961, Harwood wrote to Hope:

> I am running another poet who has appeared in *Meanjin*, *Quadrant* and the *Bully*. Can you pick me out behind the mask?

Behind this question, she seemed to be asking: do I have a poetic voice of my own? How narrow or how wide can I range and still be me? In hindsight, her multiple voices are coherent, and her decision to republish some of the pseudonymous poems in her first two books under her own name seems perfectly reasonable. It would be wrong to consider Harwood some sort of antipodean Pessoa.

Finally, it should be remembered that Harwood loved writing in character and did so very well. Her lyric and meditative bent is regularly emphasised, but she was equally a poet of short narrative and adopted voice. The Kröte poems, for example, and those of Professor Eisenbart, develop two characters whose liveliness resembles Browning:

> Kröte is drunk, but still can play.
> Knick-knacks in shadow boxes wink
> at gewgaws while he grinds away
> at Brahms, not much the worse for drink.
>
> The hostess pats her tinted curls.
> Sees, yawning surreptitiously,
> a bitch in black with ginger pearls
> squeezing the local tenor's knee.
>
> ('At the Arts Club')

The social satire and playfulness of Kröte is a world away from one of her most popular pieces, 'Barn Owl', though this too shares a narrative drive and a totally imagined scenario. Harwood explained in a letter that she had never killed an owl, unlike the first person narrator here:

> My first shot struck. He swayed,
> ruined, beating his only
> wing, as I watched, afraid
> by the fallen gun, a lonely
> child who believed death clean
> and final, not this obscene
>
> bundle of stuff that dropped,
> and dribbled through loose straw
> tangling in bowels, and hopped
> blindly closer. I saw
> those eyes that did not see
> mirror my cruelty

while the wrecked thing that could
not bear the light nor hide
hobbled in its own blood.
My father reached my side,
gave me the fallen gun.
'End what you have begun.'

A particularly interesting case in any discussion of Harwood's disguises is the poem 'The Sentry', which appeared in her first collection, *Poems* (1963), under her own name. It was written by Vincent Buckley, once again as a literary joke. According to accounts in Harwood's letters, the incident unfolded something like this. At a supper party in Hobart, Buckley was complaining about an unfavourable review Leonie Kramer had written of a book by Evan Jones. As Kramer had been appointed editor of *Australian Poetry* for that year, Buckley suggested sending in fake poems in revenge. Harwood reports the conversation thus:

> Vincent: Someone should send her some fake poems.
> Jim [McAuley]: Well I've done my share of that; no more for me after Ern Malley.
> Vincent: How about you Gwen?
> Gwen: Ok. I'll write yours for you.
> Vincent: And I'll write yours.

And so he did. Buckley's parody of Harwood's style contains such lines as:

> or perhaps the sun falling without sound
> rushed in the turning centres of his eyes
> while heat melted the snowman of his will.

So it was with a mixture of consternation and delight that she wrote to Buckley in 1962, when the poem had been accepted under her own name, not only for publication, but republication in the yearly 'best-of' anthology:

> Dear Vin,
> I don't write to importune
> or solicit attention, I swear;
> I wish to announce the good fortune
> which you, in a fashion, should share.
> Remember a poem, 'The Sentry' —
> distinguished in content and style?
> Through the gates of Aust. Lit. it made entry
> then sank to oblivion a while.
> Some heads are no bigger than buttons,
> but yours, though of usual size
> may swell: an anthology (Dutton's)
> has captured the poem as a prize.
> Is it yours? It is mine? Or the Muse's
> Whose hand drove the talented pen?
> With the right hand that never refuses
> a guinea, I signed it.
>           Yours Gwen.

I don't know what we are to make of Harwood's decision to publish it again in *Poems* (1963). A continuation of the game with Buckley, perhaps? A desire to be more closely linked to the better known poet and professor? Certainly, for a long time Harwood did not know where she stood with Buckley. She suspected that he had been responsible for pointing out the acrostic to the *Bulletin* in the first place, and then fomenting the hysteria which followed to his own advantage (he became the new poetry editor of the *Bully* not long after). They remained lifelong friends.

Thankfully, the primness of the public reaction to the So Long Bulletin hoax now seems a long way in the past, though it is debatable whether the quality of our literary editors would impress Harwood today. But until late in her life she would battle to be taken seriously as a poet, and not just a housewife dilettante with a childish voice ('my voice is a terrible handicap', she wrote in 1960), just as she would continue to struggle to find sympathetic ears for her mixture of earnestness and wicked humour. Twenty-five years after the hoax, while Harwood was in hospital, a junior doctor, who had been conferring in hushed tones with his senior colleague before entering her room, on finishing his examination boldly asked the elderly lady, 'By the way, what's an acrostic?'

\*

Harwood was born Gwendoline Nessie Foster in 1920 in Brisbane, where she spent a childhood that she liked to describe as blissfully happy. Within a few months of the end of World War Two, she married and moved to Hobart, where her husband, Bill Harwood, had just taken up a lectureship at the University of Tasmania.

Nineteen forty-five. I have been sick
all the way from Brisbane; first time in the air.
My husband's waiting in civilian clothes.
Another name now. All those burning glances
cancelled, all those raging letters burned.

('1945')

Another 21 years were to pass before she revisited the mainland, and she would live in Tasmania for the rest of her life, despite its differences from the Eden of her youth:

> I can never express my loathing for Hobart. For me the place is a creeping misery. It eats one's will away.

Harwood liked to insist that her life had been uneventful. To A. D. Hope she wrote, 'I have lived a quiet domestic life with 4 children'. But the reality is she had to juggle three careers: that of mother, that of a secretary in a doctor's surgery, and the secret one of poetry (she composed largely in her head, and her teenage daughter once declared that she had scarcely seen her mother write a line of verse). She seems to have oscillated between frustration that she did not have more time for poetry and feeling grateful for that persona of housewife, which protected her from the literary world and its cast of hyper-inflated egos.

> When people tell me I'm a genius I reach for the All-Bran. Sauce is fine but you need bulk. That kind of talk makes me nervous and eager to get behind a mask.

Mask, or reality check, the role of Tasmanian housewife had a grounding effect, but it could also offer perspective on the creative process:

> Children are better than the best poems, but poems are good too. Of course I shall always be able to write something, but technical skill is nothing without the passion of creation — 'the internal ceremony of creation'. I'm glad I have the children: they'll stop people saying, when the book comes out, 'O she'd never write all that mad stuff if she had a family to look after'.

This passage from her letters is typical in the way that it runs with various strands of thought simultaneously. If we are warranted in detecting an inherent fear of the expectations of others in the final comment, then it is even more admirable that Harwood also found ways to describe her resentment at being trapped in the role of mother, at a time when doing so was frowned upon as a sign of ingratitude. Her widely anthologised sonnet 'In the Park' describes an exhausted mother sitting on a park bench while her two children bicker around her. It ends with the line, 'To the wind she says, "They have eaten me alive"'. It is characteristic of Harwood that she played with disassociating herself from, and then embracing, these sentiments, like a yoyo that she drew in and out. It is often forgotten that 'In the Park' was first published under the name of Walter Lehmann — as if to distance it from her own voice. But in a letter to Buckley in 1962 she writes, 'I have a short time before the children come home for the May holidays and start eating me alive'. In this more intimate context, with a possible hint of irony, she can adopt the idea more readily.

Then, of course, there is her late sonnet which begins:

She sits in the park, wishing she'd never written
about that dowdy housewife and her brood.
Better, the Memoirs of a Mad Sex-Kitten
Or a high minded Ode to Motherhood
in common metre with a grand doxology.

('Later Texts')

And thus one never knows where the real Gwen Harwood stands. There is a continual shifting of roles, donning of masks, and, aided by her sharp wit, an undermining of the restrictive expectations of the society around her.

In this sense, Harwood is of her time as a modern poet. But she was also able to declare more courageously than many of her contemporaries that, 'Poetry is a way from one mind to another'. Paul Kane has noted that few poets inscribe as many poems to others as Gwen Harwood. Poems such as 'An Impromptu for Ann Jennings' and 'At Mornington' discuss recurrent themes of friendship, music and time with such a personal note, with an intimacy and (dare one say it) sincerity, that they read like private letters.

Harwood was one of Australia's great letter writers. Many readers will know her early missives to Tony Riddell from Brisbane, collected in the volume *Blessed City* (1990), but she continued to write regularly to a small circle of friends throughout her life. It is hard to underestimate the damage that may have been done to our ways of being in the world as a result of the loss of the genre of letter writing. We have so few written forums in which to reflect on ourselves to another individual, and we have become coy about signing anything 'yours sincerely' or 'truthfully' or 'whole-heartedly'. The formula that has come to dominate emails — 'best' — is vacuous by comparison, and indicative of the functional and impersonal nature of electronic correspondence. The letter, by contrast, offers a space in which to recount the quotidian nature of being, and the slow accretion of experiences and emotions that form a life. In this context, Harwood's letters stand as models, and deserve to be better known. I can't help feeling she was more at ease in this genre. Sometimes you get the impression that in her poetry the complexities involved in juggling a host of public and private personae (the Tasmanian Housewife with the childish voice quoting Wittgenstein), the name-shifting and unmasking could be a distraction. There is a clarity and concision of expression in the letters, coupled with wit and playfulness, that is very endearing. To Edwin Tanner she writes:

> I promise myself that I'll write long ones in return as soon as I have washed the dishes, but in fact I am generally so tired after dinner that I just long to curl up in Plato's cave and watch the flickering images.

It is as if she trusts her audience in a way she can never do when a poem is sent to one of those fickle editors, and then out to unknown readers. When she signs off 'yours sincerely' or 'yours with warm quixotry', you feel she means it.

'Spilling the days no memory will restore / time's fountain climbs its own perpetual core', she writes at the end of a poem called, significantly, 'A Postcard'. Against this waste, it is her letters that stand defiant. 'How little time we've spent together in the 35 years since 1942, how much time we've kept forever in our letters,' she wrote to Riddell in 1977.

*

One of the striking things about Harwood's poetry is how resistant it is to categorisation into schools or movements. She refused to be seen as a Tasmanian or Australian poet, or for that matter as a female poet: 'there's just poetry, whoever has written it'. 'One of the difficulties about being a woman poet,' she declared in an interview in 1975:

is that there is no way to address the Muse . . . it is easy for men to write poems to the Muse because she can be a kind of composite, a wife or mistress, a lover, an inspirer, but to whom do women speak?

In could be argued that one of the ways Harwood overcame this was to write from male perspectives, as she does in 'The Wine is Drunk', a post-coital meditation. Harwood wrote to Riddell about this poem, 'In the poem it is the man speaking, but of course it is my own voice on my own themes; it sounds odd in the feminine voice' — an apt description of Harwood's whole poetic endeavour, and a reminder of the limited range of personae available to female poets at the time.

> I must be absent from myself
> must learn to praise love's waking face,
> raise this unleavened heart, and sever
>
> from my true life this ignorant sorrow.
> I must in this gross darkness cherish
> more than all plenitude the hunger
> that drives the spirit. . . .

Harwood had originally called the poem 'Gradus ad Parnassum', a more characteristic title for her, with its Latin and musical overtones and its irony. Also characteristic is the use of tetrameter. Although she loosened up metrically in her later work, the majority of her poetry, and certainly her best, makes use of rhyme and either tetrameter or trimeter. Perhaps she felt the pentameter lacked the concision so common in her work. She was not afraid to declare that 'bad workmanship is quite immoral'. One should not assume from this that she was hostile to free verse, but rather that she understood how hard it is to do well: 'Really I like best to write in strict forms, but I feel that achieving creative tension in a context of liberty is a real challenge'. Quite rightly, Harwood recognised that the weakness of most free verse lies not in the lack of metre and rhyme, but in the dissipation of any creative tension when artifice is ignored.

As mentioned earlier, many of Harwood's poems are short narratives in a range of voices. Along with the Kröte and Eisenbart poems, the standouts are 'The Lion's Bride', 'A Simple Story' and 'Barn Owl'. But a meditative and lyric vein is characteristic of equally fine poems such as 'Dust to Dust' and 'At Mornington', in which an ennobling strain rallies strongly:

> and when I am seized at last
> and rolled in one grinding race
> of dreams, pain, memories, love and grief,
> from which no hand will save me,
> the peace of this day will shine
> like light on the face of the waters
> that bear me away for ever.

Perhaps this tone, and the use of big abstract nouns like time, love, memory and death, are what Harwood had in mind when she described herself as a capital-R Romantic. In Harwood, there are not many signs of the revolutionary fervour of Shelley's 'Mask of Anarchy' or (despite the frequent references to Wittgenstein) the philosophical musings of Coleridge and Wordsworth. Keats is perhaps closer to the mark. Where such a self-reflective quality combines with a steady reasoned and witty voice, it makes for some of her strongest work.

One of my favourite examples is 'Evening, Oyster Cove'. It begins simply enough with three rhyming quatrains of spirited and quirky landscape description, culminating in:

Crows, bound for Bruny. Wingbeats make
the sound of runners breathing, in

their firm compacted paths of air.
Sunset pours golden syrup on
the northern sandstone. Treetops flare
briefly, and then the sun is gone.

How often in Australian poetry are such descriptions an end in themselves that bear out the epitaph from Wittgenstein appended to this poem, 'What is history to me? Mine is the first and only world'? What I love about 'Evening, Oyster Cove' is the way Harwood moves between this personal descriptive realm, in which:

My geese call from the western rise —
Babydoll, Fido, Stagolee —
the haunting wildness of their cries
mocks well-fed domesticity,

and finds herself in an historical plain that encompasses the early painters, and then the original inhabitants of the land:

This elbow of the shallow bay
crooked an unchilded dying race
whose liquid language ebbed away.
Shadows forgather in this place:

before returning to muse on the narrator's sense of guilt for the past:

... The sea's
a sheet of melancholy light.
Herons half made of shadow seize

their meal, like necromancers search
obscuring crystal for a sign.
My boat grounds gently on the beach.
Home to books, fire and chilled white wine.

Ghosts of the night mist, set me free.
Forgive, until the past is called
wisdom, and history can be
told in some last redeeming world.

I hope I am correct in detecting a note of irony when the narrator asks the ghosts of the past to forgive and set her free to enjoy such worldly pleasures as books and white wine. You are never quite sure with Harwood.

*

It is a sign of the maturity of a society that it should want to incorporate the past rather than reject it. Much of our poetic culture is focussed on the contemporary moment, on the winners and losers of the latest prize or fellowship, on seeking out a new star who will save poetry from irrelevance. In this narrow context editors and publishers who have the magnanimity to widen their gaze, who aim to recuperate and reinstate, who are not afraid to challenge the present by setting it against the authors who came before us, deserve our congratulations. In recent years the efforts of some Australian publishers to rerelease unduly neglected authors is admirable. In the field of poetry the

University of Western Australia Press stands out here, with their editions of Lesbia Harford, John Shaw Neilson, Francis Webb and Dorothy Hewett. If you think contemporary poets struggle to find a publisher and generate sales, the scenario is even more dire for the deceased, who have a hard time promoting themselves from the grave.

In the case of a selective anthology such as this new book, *The Best 100 Poems of Gwen Harwood*, both the adjective and the magical number have a trace of the ludicrous. One would like to think that Harwood had reached a level of importance where gratuitous boosting was unnecessary. What I find particularly odd about this new edition is the fact that the name of the selector and compiler is not to be found in the book itself. John Harwood, an academic and novelist, and Gwen Harwood's son, is only acknowledged in such a role on the inside of the dust jacket. There is no introduction or editorial note, and no list of Harwood's publications. Only a summary biographical note is included on the dust jacket, and even an alphabetical list of titles or first lines has been considered redundant. One is led to believe that the best 100 poems had something of divine revelation about them. They require no paratext to justify the selection, or aid the reader encountering the poetry for the first time. They just are and ever shall be thus.

The standard edition of Harwood's work is *Collected Poems 1943–1995*, edited by Alison Hoddnott and Gregory Kratzmann (UQP, 2003). It contains the six published volumes, along with a good sway of uncollected material (though not 'The Sentry', nor some of the light verse found in *A Steady Storm of Correspondence: Selected Letters of Gwen Harwood*, also edited by Gregory Kratzmann (UQP, 2001)). There have been a number of selections of Harwood's poetry already. A 1992 Angus and

Robertson (or Anguish and Robbery as Harwood and Buckley liked to say) volume is out of print, but a Penguin edition from 2001 still seems to be available as an e-book. There is also a fine recent selection by Chris Wallace-Crabbe and Gregory Kratzmann, *Mappings of the Plane: New Selected Poems*, published in 2009 by Carcanet. The present volume holds its own against the previous ones in terms of selection. It is similar in length to *Mappings of the Plane*, and, like its predecessor, gives a good sense of Harwood's range and strengths. However, the irksome presentation makes it very difficult to see who would benefit from *The Best 100 Poems*. One can't help thinking it would only have reinforced Harwood's disdain for publishers, and one wonders whether, if we lend an ear, we might once more make out that high-pitched voice calling from the grave, 'Fuck all editors'.

## Works Cited

Gwen Harwood, *Blessed City: The Letters of Gwen Harwood to Thomas Riddell, January to September 1943*, edited by Alison Hoddinott, Angus and Robertson, 1990.

Gwen Harwood, *A Steady Storm of Correspondence: Selected Letters of Gwen Harwood*, edited by Gregory Kratzmann, University of Queensland Press, 2001.

Gwen Harwood, *Collected Poems 1943–1995*, edited by Alison Hoddnott and Gregory Kratzmann, University of Queensland Press, 2003.

Gwen Harwood, *Mappings of the Plane: New Selected Poems*, edited by Chris Wallace-Crabbe and Gregory Kratzmann, Carcanet, 2009.

Gwen Harwood, *The Best 100 Poems of Gwen Harwood*, Black Inc, 2014.

# Auden's Skirmish
# with the Real

Our earth in 1969
Is not the planet I call mine,
The world, I mean, that gives me strength
To hold off chaos at arm's length.

My Eden landscapes and their climes
Are constructs from Edwardian times,
When bath-rooms took up lots of space,
And, before eating, one said Grace.

So begins W. H. Auden's late poem 'Doggerel by a Senior Citizen', though doggerel is hardly an accurate description of what is a carefully composed piece in regular metre. There is a video recording of the author reciting it from memory for a television chat program. He was sixty-two at the time. He looks like a fish out of water — his generously wrinkled face, his voice quiet and stately. Unfazed by the context, he gives each word a gravitas that belies the comic verse form and the intimate tone.

The poem does not shy away from making pronouncements. One feels it aims to embody no less than society's conscience:

Sex was, of course — it always is —
The most enticing of mysteries,
But news-stands did not yet supply
Manichaean pornography.

Then Speech was mannerly, an Art,
Like learning not to belch or fart:
I cannot settle which is worse,
The Anti-Novel or Free Verse.

before concluding with a challenge to those who might be quick to dismiss the author as out of touch:

Me alienated? Bosh! It's just
As a sworn citizen who must
Skirmish with it that I feel
Most at home with what is Real.

That last stanza lifts the poem way beyond the realms of doggerel, and reminds us that its author was not merely a grumpy old man, but still one of the sharpest writers of his age. How was it that Auden could be, as Edward Mendelson describes him in the introduction to two new volumes of Auden's prose, both the most universal of modern poets and the most individual? What did it mean for Auden to be a 'sworn citizen' who must skirmish with the Real?

*Prose, Volume V, 1963–1968*, and *Prose, Volume VI, 1969–1973*, comprise the final two volumes of the collected prose of Auden published by Princeton University Press under the exemplary editorship of Edward Mendelson. They cover the last ten years of the poet's life, from 1963 through to 1973 when he died at the age of sixty-six. They contain material well-known to readers, such as *A Certain World*, the T. S. Eliot lectures, *Secondary Worlds*, and some of the essays that would make up *Forewords and Afterwords*. But there is also much previously uncollected and some previously unpublished material. Auden had based himself in New York since 1939, having left, or as some back home had seen it, abandoned England shortly before the outbreak of World War II, and he had been an American citizen since 1946. Since 1957 he spent each summer in a house he had bought outside Vienna, and in his final years was a more regular visitor to England. Auden's poetic creations in this period comprise *About the House* (1965) and *City without Walls* (1969), then *Epistle to a Grandson* (1972) and the posthumous *Thank You, Fog* (1974). Some would say Auden's greatest poetry was already behind him. But it would be wrong to focus on the light and occasional verse which became more frequent in these last years. It is a period in which he experimented widely with verse forms and metres. There are also key works, 'Thanksgiving for a Habitat', for example, a sequence of poems on the various rooms of his house in Austria. As he wrote to Christopher Isherwood of this sequence, though it could be characteristic of much of his late poetry, 'for the first time I have felt old enough and sure enough of myself to speak in my own person'.

In his prose he had already confidently found such a voice much earlier. For Auden the writing of literary non-fiction prose, which largely consists of reviews, prefaces, and lectures, was far from hack work. America allowed Auden to make a living as a freelance prose writer, and he took the job very seriously. The two volumes in question total well over a thousand pages. It is striking how consistently measured and thoughtful each piece is.

He may repeat ideas in different forums, but you never have the sense that he is rushing for a deadline, or that he ever was rash in his judgement or expression. In these last two volumes we learn a little more of his personal life, particularly his childhood, and there are discussions on homosexuality, and the occasional reflective comment on his own poetry ('I have always thought about myself as a comic poet', he writes in 1971). But it is his clarity of thought in describing our age of anxiety that gives his prose such lasting weight.

*

As I read these pieces I found myself less concerned with Auden's insights on particular authors, and very much interested in his general ideas about art and society. One of the refreshing things about Auden is the way he wrote outwards, trying to encapsulate the specific in the universal. Reviewing and essay writing by the fifties had become Auden's way to reach a wider public. Freelance work was his pulpit or lectern. He made a rule for himself only to write on books he generally liked. There were limits to his freedom, but two striking examples suggest that he stuck by his principles. In 1966 he was commissioned by *Life* magazine to write an essay on the end of the Roman Empire for $10,000, a tidy amount even today. But when he refused to recast the ending, which the editors had found too pessimistic, the piece was rejected. Here are the concluding two paragraphs:

> I think a great many of us are haunted by the feeling that our society, and by ours I don't mean just the United States or Europe, but our whole world-wide technological civilization, whether officially labelled capitalist, socialist or communist, is going to go smash, and probably deserves to.

Like the third century the twentieth is an age of stress and anxiety. In our case, it is not that our techniques are too primitive
to cope with new problems, but the very fantastic success of
our technology is creating a hideous, noisy, over-crowded world
in which it is becoming increasingly difficult to lead a human
life. In our reactions to this, one can see many parallels to the
third century. Instead of gnostics, we have existentialists and
God-is-dead theologians, instead of neo-platonists, devotees of
Zen, instead of desert hermits, heroin addicts and beats (who
also, oddly enough, seem adverse to washing), instead of mor-
tification of the flesh, sado-masochistic pornography; as for our
public entertainments, the fare offered by television is still a
shade less brutal and vulgar than that provided by the amphi-
theatre, but only a shade, and may not be for long.

A second story is already well known, but is now described in
more detail by Mendelson. It relates to Auden's refusal to change
his introduction to the English edition of Dag Hammarskjöld's
*Markings*, which is said to have cost him the 1964 Nobel Prize.
Auden had been Hammarskjöld's choice for the award before
his death. In 1963, when it was won by George Seferis, Auden
was one of three finalists, and was widely expected to get up
the following year. In the spring of that year Hammarskjöld's
executors and friends in the diplomatic service were said to have
been 'horrified and offended' by Auden's introduction when
they read it in typescript. As Edward Mendelson recounts in his
own introduction:

> A high Swedish official visited Auden in New York and hinted
> that the Swedish Academy would be distressed if his introduc-
> tion should be printed as written. Auden refused to rewrite it,
> and, that evening, said to his friend Lincoln Kirstein, "There
> goes the Nobel Prize."

\*

Auden, more lucidly than most, was able to identify and describe characteristics of the cultural malaise that continues to resonate forty years after his death. Too many aspects of modern life isolate us within our subjective selves. As a result it becomes difficult to believe in the reality of other people. Fragmentation, a lack of encounters with the sacred, and a monotone impressionism characterize much of our artistic production. In verse of the last sixty years the result has been a hyper-subjectivity in two polarized forms of hermeticism and confessionalism. In the face of such a situation, Auden argued, 'Art can only have one subject — man as a conscious unique person'. The characteristic hero of our age is not the great man, or the romantic rebel, but the humble individual on a 'quest for authenticity':

> Everybody who lives in a technological civilization (and in the West we have lived in one for a century and a half), is in constant danger of ceasing to be himself — ceasing to be even a member of a certain nation, class, or profession and becoming an anonymous unit of the public.

And yet Auden is also a self-effacing writer, and rarely autobiographical. When he writes, 'The only proper resistance is the cultivation of a dispassionate passion to see things as they are and to remember what really happened', we understand that his *self* must raise itself out of the extremes of subjectivism, if necessary by its bootstraps, and *be* in relation to others. The result was Auden's great civic poetry. In talking of his art in these pieces he returns to the metaphor of a community — as opposed to that inchoate crowd the public:

> The subject matter of a poem is comprised of a crowd of recollected occasions of feeling, among which the most important are recollections of encounters with sacred beings or events. This crowd the poet attempts to transform into a community by embodying it in a verbal society.

Because poetry is made from the stuff of language, and words are a product of human society, they embody the ideal not only of communication but of community. If, as Auden wrote, a poet 'is, before everything else, a person who is passionately in love with language', then he is also necessarily a believer in the possibility of human love more widely. In a well-known phrase from *The Dyer's Hand* Auden expressed this as follows:

> Poetry can do a hundred and one things, delight, sadden, disturb, amuse, instruct — it may express every possible shade of emotion, and describe every conceivable kind of event, but there is only one thing that all poetry must do; it must praise all it can for being and for happening.

The cumulative power of such thoughts is an eloquent defence of something we have almost forgotten: the moral importance of poetry.

\*

Many of these ideas were formulated by Auden prior to 1963, and resurface repeatedly in his last ten years. However the last decade also saw the development of important new ideas. Characteristically for Auden, they came to be expressed as dichotomies: Nowness and Permanence, and later Primary and Secondary Worlds. I will present these ideas by quoting generously from Auden himself, who once said that ideally a review should consist entirely of carefully selected passages from the book in question.

Auden had long been describing the modern hero's struggle to become a unique person. He was now, however, more and more concerned to distinguish between two modes of expressing that struggle: personal utterance and self-expression.

> The experience an artist attempts to embody is of a reality common to all, and only his in that it is perceived from a perspective which nobody but he can occupy. He will never succeed in creating a satisfactory work, unless he can master his narcissism and learn to look at his experience with complete detachment, as if it were somebody else's.

Personal utterance requires one to embody the individual in the universal. Self-expression on the other hand tends to forget our common reality by focussing inwards. One can sense Auden taking aim at confessionalist poets 'petrified by their gorgon egos', as he wrote in 'Ode to the Medieval Poets'.

The focus on self-expression in contemporary poetry is often accompanied by a preference for Nowness over Permanence. In Auden's scheme, Permanence is a quality which can only be found by bringing the personal experience clearly into the universal domain.

> Every genuine work of art exhibits two qualities, Nowness — an art-historian can assign at least an approximate date to its making — and Permanence — it remains on hand in the world long after its maker and his society have ceased to exist.

Auden swam against the tide in emphasising the importance of the second of these terms. His example of Nowness is limited to the art historian who will focus on technical aspects needed to date a work, rather than on the individual's self-expression or display of originality. Time and again he celebrates the quality of Permanence as an ideal for poetic creation. He points out that in art there is no such thing as progress, and political terms like conservative or radical are meaningless. One art work does not supersede its predecessors in the way a new government or scientific discovery may. Rather the artist hopes 'to make something which will endure and, in due time, take its permanent place in the tradition'. The visual image of this might be Raphael's Parnassus fresco in the Vatican. As he wrote in the poem 'Shorts II', *'What should I write at sixty-four?* is a question, a folly / *What should I write in Nineteen-Hundred-and-Seventy-One?'*. This idea was repeated in numerous contexts in the prose, where it is more fleshed out:

'What sort of poetry should I write at the age of sixty-five' is a sensible question, but to ask 'what should I write in the year 1972?' is sheer folly. It can only result in submission to the fashion of the moment, a desperate attempt to be 'with it'. Plato tried to model political life on artistic fabrication: this as we know, can only lead to political tyranny. The error made by all too many artists today is the exact opposite: they try to model artistic fabrication on political action so that, instead of trying to make an artistic object of permanent value, they surrender to the tyranny of the immediate moment and produce meaningless 'happenings'.

This idea led to two criticisms by Auden of his contemporaries which seem equally pertinent today. Firstly, that the desire for originality in art, however attractive it may seem in our hyper-consumerist society, is a chimera:

Only pseudo-artists bother their heads about being original. To think consciously of being original is to have one's eye fixed not upon the work to be made but upon the works of others, one's efforts centred upon not doing what others have done or are doing, instead of upon what one should be doing oneself; and the result is most certain to be fake.

The consumption of art is also damaging:

We are all of us tempted to read more books, look at more pictures, listen to more music, than we can possibly absorb; and the result of such gluttony is not a cultured mind but a consuming one; what it reads, looks at, listens to, is immediately forgotten, leaving no more traces behind it than yesterday's newspaper. The focus on nowness leads in short to a situation where 'the work of art is a random happening, which neither the artist or the public are expected to interpret or judge; all they can do is register that it has occurred.

The second criticism concerns the danger of confusing poetry and political action. This relates to the point expressed in the passage above regarding Plato, but again it is worth quoting in full:

By all means let a poet, if he wants to, write an *engagé* poem, protesting against this or that social evil or injustice, so long as he doesn't imagine that it will alter anything: the person who will most profit from it is himself, for it will enhance his literary reputation among those who feel the same as he does. In trying to improve the world only two things are effective, political action and straight journalistic reportage of the facts. The poet, qua poet, has only one political duty: by his own example, to try to preserve the purity of language against corruption and

misuse, for, when words lose their meaning, then physical force
gives the orders

Auden correctly identifies how the peril of self-expression lies in
its tendency to draw us away from reality.

> I may be wrong but I think we are nearing the end of a period
> in which the philosophers and scientists were convinced that
> the 'reality' behind appearances was a soulless mechanism; and
> the artists, in reaction, rejected the phenomenal world in favour
> of the cultivation of their subjective emotions — an attitude
> summed up by Blake's statement: 'some people see the sun as a
> round disk the size of a guinea, but I see it as a host crying Holy,
> Holy, Holy', in which he denies all value to what his physical
> eyes see . . .

If Blake stands near the beginning of that subjective tradition,
and is often seen as one of its most positive embodiments, it was
the twentieth century which taught us the dangers of subjectivism, as Auden described in one of his best poems of this period,
'The Cave of Making':

> More than ever
> life-out-there is goodly, miraculous, loveable,
> but we shan't, not since Stalin and Hitler,
> trust ourselves ever again: we know that subjectively,
> all is possible.

This reminds me of the chapter in Primo Levi's *The Periodic
Table* called 'Uranium', in which the narrator meets Bonino, a
man who happily invents fanciful stories of his heroic exploits
during the war, while oblivious to the harrowing experiences of
his interlocutor. And yet, it still requires a certain courage to

invoke such ideals as truth in today's world where we are urged to valorise our personal interpretation or experience of events over the event itself: 'how was it for *you?*', we ask, 'how did it make *you* feel?'. As Auden wrote in the poem 'Plains' from the sequence *Bucolics*:

> nothing is lovely,
> not even in poetry, which is not the case.

A poet must never make a statement simply because it sounds poetically exciting, he wrote. This famously led him to change the ending of a much loved poem, 'September 1, 1939', and then to disown the poem completely. As he recounts in one of the pieces collected here:

> Rereading a poem of mine, '1st September, 1939' after it had been published, I came to the line
> We must love one another or die
> and said to myself: 'that's a damned lie! We must die anyway'.
> So, in the next edition, I altered it to
> We must love one another and die.
> This didn't seem to do either, so I cut the stanza. Still no good. The whole poem, I realized, was infected with an incurable dishonesty and must be scrapped.

\*

The importance of reaffirming our relation to reality in art, and of speaking honestly, led Auden in the sixties to formulate another major idea of his late prose: the distinction between primary and secondary worlds. It was a theme that allowed him to bring the tensions of nowness and permanence into a harmonious rapport. Auden took the terms from J. R. R. Tolkien, and first used in the title to his T. S. Eliot lectures published in 1969 as *Secondary Worlds*. The primary world is that of reality common to all of us. The secondary world is that fictive and mythic world each artist creates. On another level, of course, the secondary world is also the world of language, at one remove from reality. However, each secondary world must aim to be faithful to the primary world, from which it draws its material and spirit.

> The initial impulse to create a secondary world is a feeling of awe aroused by encounters, in the Primary World, with sacred beings or events. This feeling of awe is an imperative, that is to say, one is not free to choose the object or the event that arouses it. Though every work of art is a Secondary World, it cannot be constructed ex nihilo, but is a selection from and a recombination of the contents of the Primary World.

On a number of occasions Auden returned to describe a game he played as a child, which must have been a formative activity in his artistic development, the construction of an imaginary lead-mining community. It bears many similarities to the elaborate horse-racing games Gerald Murnane describes repeatedly in his fiction.

> Most of what I know about the writing of poetry, or at least about the kind I am interested in writing, I discovered long before I took any interest in poetry itself. Between the ages of six and twelve, I spent a great many of my waking hours in the fabrication of a private secondary sacred world, the basic elements of which were (a) a limestone landscape mainly derived from the Pennine Moors in the North of England, and (b) an industry — lead-mining. . . . As regards my particular lead-mining world, I decided, or rather, without conscious decision, I instinctively felt that I must impose two restrictions

upon my freedom of fantasy. In choosing what objects were to
be included, I was free to select this and reject that, on condition that both were real objects in the primary world, to choose,
for example, between two kinds of water turbine, . . . I was not
allowed to invent one.

Auden goes on to describe how at a certain point in this game
he made a key discovery about his secondary world which was
to have implications for his poetry, and particularly the choice
exemplified in the rejection of 'September 1, 1939'.

As I was planning my Platonic Idea of a concentrating mill,
I ran into difficulties. I had to choose between two types of a
certain machine for separating the slimes, called a buddle. One
type I found more sacred or 'beautiful', but the other type was,
as I knew from my reading, the more efficient. At this point
I realized that it was my moral duty to sacrifice my aesthetic
preference to reality or truth.

When in 1970 Auden compiled his commonplace book, which
he thought of as a sort of self-portrait, he returned to the secondary world idea, by naming it *A Certain World*. The book is made
up of quotations from other writers and short reflections by the
author arranged under headings and presented alphabetically.
The final heading, 'Writing', concludes with the description of
Auden's lead-mining world quoted above, followed by a repeti-
tion of the distinction between self-expression and the unique
perspective on a common reality; and then finally this quotation
from St Augustine:

The truth is neither mine nor his nor another's; but belongs to
us all whom Thou callest to partake of it, warning us terribly,
not to account it private to ourselves, lest we be deprived of it.

The idea of the creative tension between the primary and secondary worlds and our need to remain open to that common reality
finds concise expression once again in 'The Cave of Making',
and goes to show how the preoccupations of Auden's prose and
poetry were very close:

> . . . I should like to become, if possible,
>     a minor Atlantic Goethe,
> with his passion for weather and stones but without his silliness
>     re the Cross: at times a bore, but,
> while knowing Speech can at best, a shadow echoing
>     the silent light, bear witness
> to the Truth it is not, he wished it were, as the francophil
>     gaggle of pure songsters
> are too vain to. . . .

*

'To bear witness to the Truth it is not' might be a neat description of Auden's poetics. In both his poetry and prose I have the
sense that personal experience has been translated into a universal form. Earlier I described this as writing outwards from
the self. Auden might have called it, keeping the secondary
world close to the primary. It sounds obvious, but when our
hold on the primary world is so tendentious it is easy to lose the
clear-sightedness of the maxim and to focus on our subjective
selves. His work in this period is characterised by the aphorism.
He didn't have much time for Latin literature apart from Horace,
but the Latin moralists such as Seneca were doing something
similar in their *sententiae*. When Dante evoked 'moral Seneca'
in the Middle Ages the adjective still had that positive sense of
manifesting high principles for leading a good life. Today more
often than not literature aims at diversion and illusion. We are

59

quick to see the negative side of moralism: its prescriptiveness and its reluctance to accentuate the subtle differences of individual experience. We hear *authority* and think *authoritarian*. But as Seneca himself wrote, in words that recall St Augustine above, 'Truth is open to all, it has not been pre-empted. Much of it is left for future generations'.

Auden was a lover of the aphorism, and in many ways the maxim characterises his prose style. The aphorism is so difficult to master because, unlike most criticism which focusses on details, and most theories which tend to abstraction, it must be concrete while convincing every reader that it is 'either universally true or true of every member of the class to which it refers, irrespective of the reader's convictions', as he wrote in the Foreword to *The Viking Book of Aphorisms* in 1962. The link to moralism is complex, however. The aphorism does not tell us how we should live, but points out how we do live. Like Auden's prose, it is descriptive rather than prescriptive.

Auden doesn't often discuss his own poetics directly in these volumes, but there is one revealing comment that stuck in my mind. He writes, 'The ideal at which I aim is a style which shall combine the drab sober truthfulness of prose with a poetic uniqueness of expression'. His essays are certainly full of a sober truthfulness, but they also contain a uniqueness of expression. In a well-known passage from 'The Cave of Making' he wrote of poetry:

> . . . After all, it's rather a privilege
>    amid the affluent traffic
> to serve this unpopular art which cannot be turned into
>    background noise for study
> or hung as a status-trophy by rising executives,
>    cannot be 'done' like Venice

> or abridged like Tolstoy, but stubbornly still insists upon
>   being read or ignored . . .

I like to think this might equally be true of much of his prose.

## Works Cited

W. H. Auden, *Prose Volume V 1963–1968*, and *Prose Volume VI 1969–1973*, ed. Edward Mendelson, Princeton University Press, 2015.

# The World is but a Word

Steward: O my good Lord, the world is but a word.
Were it all yours to give it in a breath,
How quickly were it gone.
Timon: You tell me true.
*(Timon of Athens)*

As a rule poets find it difficult to describe their work. In answering the question *what do you write about?*, novelists will happily speak of the characters who inhabit their worlds. But poets, unless they compose polemics or verse novels, are at a loss. If they invoke anything to do with their own feelings, or way of experiencing the world, they fear being dismissed as a neo-romantic. If they mention the words *love* and *nature*, they are certain people will start throwing stones. For a long time I tried to avoid this predicament by declaring curtly that I wrote about language. Like Timon and his Steward in the exchange above, I felt that poetry was primarily, almost exclusively, a question of words, and that reality was as fragile as the language we use to describe it. I have come to believe this a limiting notion, and potentially dangerous. So what might poetry be about?

The task of the poet is to scrutinize the actual world. Where we proclaim the world is but a word, or a dream, or an interpretation, our literature struggles to be more than a patina of the poet's moods. We lose sight of our relations to other individuals and to things. A healthy relationship with the world is a two-way circuit, in which a shared reality both enriches and checks the perspective of the individual. Poetry is animated by this sense of encounter. These encounters can take place in the turbulent social arena Shakespeare conjures at the start of *Timon of Athens*, but they can also include our experiences of the natural world.

There is a common perception that poetry turns to the natural world in search of an idyllic escape from, or a simplification of, our social existences. This is not the case. Or where it is, Nature soon offers a powerful reality check. In our encounters with Demeter we are further from our comfort zones and the comfort zone of our language. We are also further from our competing subjective points of view. Instead we are forced to see things as they are. Nature, as Apemanus reminds Timon, is that which doesn't flatter man or heed his self-importance:

. . . What thinks't
that the bleak air, thy boisterous chamberlain
will put thy shirt on warm? Will these moist trees,
that have out-lived the eagle, page thy heels
and skip when thou point'st out? Will the cold brook
candied with ice, caudle thy morning taste
to cure thy o'er-night's surfeit? Call the creatures,
whose naked natures live in all the spite
of wreakful Heaven, whose bare unhoused trunks,

to the conflicting elements expos'd
answer mere Nature: bid them flatter thee.

Heraclitus is recorded as having said that there is a single common universe for those who are awake. It is in sleep that each of us turns away into our own private worlds. The nature I am invoking so imprecisely is that common universe of things and facts. We tend to portray it as distinct from the human realm in order to delimit all that *is* socially determined and subjective. On some level, of course, this is a misconception, and yet we continue to isolate ourselves. It's not simply a trace of our cultural heritage, in which man was the measure of all things, and at the top of a god-given hierarchy. There is no denying we are a singular creation within Gaia's realm. As individuals, however, we tend in two directions: towards detachment, in order to see ourselves more clearly; and towards unity, in order not to be alone. In our quest to be authentic and integral individuals, the perspective of nature keeps our subjective selves rooted in wider realities and helps us to feel that we might be integral to something larger than ourselves. There is something of this in Wordsworth's notion of sense sublime:

> . . . And I have felt
> A presence that disturbs me with the joy
> Of elevated thoughts; a sense sublime
> Of something far more deeply interfused,
> Whose dwelling is the light of setting suns,
> And the round ocean and the living air,
> And the blue sky, and in the mind of man;
> A motion and a spirit, that impels
> All thinking things, all objects of all thought,
> And rolls through all things.

Wordsworth emphasises the commonality of thinking things and objects of thought through the repeated adjective 'all' in this passage from 'Lines Composed a Few Miles above Tintern Abbey'.

Writing poetry is a way of questioning and positing our being in the world. Auden writes in 'Precious 5', 'There is a world to see: / Look outward, eyes, and love / Those eyes you cannot be.' But looking outwards with a heart disposed to love is a difficult quest. We are interrogated by external realities and our dealings with other people. It would be easier to retreat within our subjective selves, and to behave as if poetry could be a self-centred activity, but then we atrophy. At the other extreme, equally fruitless, are those attempts to shun all personal sentiment and the first person pronoun.

Positing our being in the world is destabilizing. While Wordsworth rallies us to uphold a belief in the ideal union of man with the presence and spirit of Nature, other poets show us the irony inherent in the word *individual*, a word whose etymology means 'that which cannot be divided'. Andrew Marvell's 'A Dialogue between the Soul and the Body' gives wonderful expression to this divide. A precursor to Marvell is Guido Cavalcanti who championed the term *sbigottimento*. *Sbigottimento* describes the shock and disorientation that the individual feels when destabilized by a powerful encounter with the external world. In the poetry of Cavalcanti and his contemporaries that experience is usually provoked by Love. But it is the *sbigottimento* rather than love that is the fulcrum of his poems, including the sonnet 'Tu m'hai sì piena di dolor la mente', the sestet of which is as follows:

*I' vo come colui ch'è fuor di vita,*
*che pare, a chi lo sguarda, ch'omo sia*

*fatto di rame o di pietra o di legno,*
*che si conduca sol per maestria*
*e porti ne lo core una ferita*
*che sia, com' egli è morto, aperto segno.*

I am held in a state of lifelessness
as one who seems to be of human kind,
likened from stuff of copper, wood, or stone,
moved to semblance by man's artifice,
who bears a wound within his heart as sign
that how he died be ever after known.

Cavalcanti often expresses a schizoid experience of the world
that is common to our own era: a lack of temporal continuity, an
identity which is continuously under threat of dissolving in its
encounters with other people; an individuality that *is* subject to
division. Italo Calvino describes something similar in the following passage from chapter two of his novel *Il cavaliere inesistente*:

> *A quell'ora dell'alba, Agilulfo aveva sempre bisogno d'applicarsi a*
> *un esercizio d'esattezza: contare oggetti, ordinarli in figure geomet-*
> *riche, risolvere problemi d'aritmetica. è l'ora in cui le cose perdono*
> *la consistenza d'ombra che le ha accompagnate nella notte e riac-*
> *quistano poco a poco i colori, ma intanto attraversano come un*
> *limbo incerto, appena sfiorate e quasi alonate dalla luce: l'ora in*
> *cui meno si è sicuri dell'esistenza del mondo. Agilulfo, lui, aveva*
> *sempre bisogno di sentirsi di fronte le cose come un muro mas-*
> *siccio al quale contrapporre la tensione della sua volontà, e solo*
> *così riusciva a mantenere una sicura coscienza di sé. Se invece il*
> *mondo intorno sfumava nell'incerto, nell'ambiguo, anch'egli si sen-*
> *tiva annegare in questa morbida penombra, non riusciva più a far*
> *affiorare dal vuoto un pensiero distinto, uno scatto di decisione,*
> *un puntiglio. Stava male: erano quelli i momenti in cui si sentiva*

*venir meno; alle volte solo a costo di uno sforzo estremo riusciva a
non dissolversi Allora si metteva a contare . . .*

Each dawn Agilulfo found he needed to apply himself to some
exercise in exactitude: counting objects, ordering them in geo-
metric shapes, solving mathematical problems. Dawn is the
moment in which things lose the shadowy consistency they
held during the night, and begin to take on colour. But before
they do so, they must cross a sort of limbo where they seem
merely brushed by light, or its halo. This is the moment when
one is least sure of the existence of the world. Agilulfo needed
to know that things before him were there like a thick wall to
which he could oppose his straining will. So when the world
around him clouded with uncertainty, he too felt engulfed in
this soft half-light, this void from which he was unable to give
rise to a single thought, or set his mind to anything. He was
tormented. These were the moments when he felt least real. At
times it was only through an extreme effort of will that he kept
himself from dissolving. And so he set to counting . . .

Counting, or ordering, are both activities associated with writing. Like Calvino, Cavalcanti was very aware of what lies behind
or beyond the ordering of reality in a poem. Yet they both
remind us that there is no escaping responsibility for the voice or
voices of that composition. The most interesting poems are occasions, passionate encounters with the here and now of the world,
rooms of language where others may dwell briefly. Of course the
vision of poetry is an imperfect one. The objects around us are
continually changing, as is the language we use to make connections. We are never whole. Or, as Timon declares while stoically
musing on death late in Shakespeare's play, only 'nothing brings
me all things'.

## Works Cited

Italo Calvino, *Il cavaliere inesistente*, in *Romanzi e racconti*, ed. C. Milanini, Mondadori, 1991.

Guido Cavalcanti, *The Selected Poetry of Guido Cavalcanti*, trans. Simon West, Troubador, 2009.

Heraclitus, *On the Universe*, trans. W. H. S. Jones, Loeb Classical Library, Harvard University Press, 1989.

Andrew Marvell, *Complete Poetry*, ed. George de F. Lord, Dent, 1984.

William Shakespeare, *Timon of Athens*, Cambridge University Press, 2000.

William Wordsworth, *Poems*, selected by Seamus Heaney, Ecco, 1988.

# As If We Were God's Spies:
# Poetry Out of Nothing

.................................................................................

*King Lear* opens with a very dramatic scene. An old man has summoned his three daughters and is about to divide his kingdom between them. First, however, he asks them to declare the strength of their filial love. Regan and Goneral speak eloquently. Then Lear asks his favourite daughter what she has to say for herself.

> *Cordelia*: Nothing, my lord.
> *Lear*: Nothing!
> *Cordelia*: Nothing.
> *Lear*: Nothing will come of nothing: speak again.

My starting point is that phrase, nothing will come of nothing, and the question, where does poetry come from? It is common to trace *nothing will come of nothing* to Lucretius and the Latin dictum *ex nihilo nihil fit* (*De rerum natura*, Book 1, ll.148–9). Lear speaks an admonition to Cordelia, but originally the maxim, which Lucretius derived from Greek tradition, was used in a positive sense to argue for the permanence of life. Everything in existence must derive from other matter already in existence. Men might be afraid, Lucretius argues, because things happen whose cause they cannot understand. They attribute these to the action of gods. However, such things are not created by divine agency out of nothing. Rather there is an eternal stock of matter from which things continually arise and to which they must eventually return. Marcus Aurelius stoically says something similar in his *Meditations*:

> I consist of a formal element and a material. Neither of these can ever pass away into nothing, any more than either of them came into being from nothing. Consequently every part of me will one day be refashioned, by a process of transition, into some other portion of the universe; which in its turn will again be changed into yet another part, and so onward to infinity. (Book V, 13).

Shakespeare, on the other hand, has Lear use the phrase as a rebuke: if you can offer nothing you will receive nothing in return. Cordelia's inability to heave her heart into her mouth sets in motion the calamities of the play, and part of that very tragedy derives from the fact that the reader knows her *nothing* to be more pregnant with love and charity, her silence to resound with more life than the glib and oily art of her sisters. It is a rough and ready knowledge, unsatisfactory for a philosopher perhaps, but serviceable enough, especially when given convincing voice in the good sense of Kent or the starkness of the Fool. For whether one agrees with Lucretius or not, on one level all life and all art are born of nothing. I did not exist and now I do. The page was empty, and now it contains a poem. It is this miracle of coming to have a form and substance that I like to think poetry should continue to celebrate.

In 'Frost at Midnight', that meditation on a winter's night as Coleridge watches his newborn son sleeping, it is just this miracle of creation out of nothing that the poet celebrates:

> The Frost performs its secret ministry,
> Unhelped by any wind. The owlet's cry
> Came loud—and hark, again! loud as before.

I have always been struck by those words 'secret ministry'. To me they evoke that sense of awe at seeing snowfall. There may be perfectly good scientific explanations for snow and frost, and yet often the sight of them returns the viewer to a state of childish wonder, as if they came out of nowhere. 'Frost at Midnight' is full of such amazement. For this reason it might be a good example of what Keats called Negative Capability. Ironically so, because in explaining the concept Keats distanced himself from poets like Coleridge:

> Negative Capability, that is, when a man is capable of being in uncertainties, mysteries, doubts, without any irritable reaching after fact and reason — Coleridge, for instance, would let go by a fine isolated verisimilitude caught from the Penetralium of mystery, from being incapable of remaining content with half-knowledge. (From a letter dated 21st Dec. 1817.)

'Frost at Midnight' celebrates at least three distinct but related mysteries or examples of half-knowledge. If the first is the frost of the title, the second is the birth of Coleridge's first child:

> Dear Babe, that sleepest cradled by my side,
> Whose gentle breathings, heard in this deep calm,

Fill up the interspersèd vacancies
And momentary pauses of the thought!

The interspersed vacancies, the void, are now full of the breath-ings of a child who until recently did not exist. What better example of *creatio ex nihilo*.

The third mystery of the poem is the film which flutters on the grate. Popularly called 'strangers', these particles of soot that dance in the heat of the fireplace were said in folklore to portend the arrival of some absent friend:

Only that film, which fluttered on the grate,
Still flutters there, the sole unquiet thing.
Methinks, its motion in this hush of nature
Gives it dim sympathies with me who live,
Making it a companionable form,
Whose puny flaps and freaks the idling Spirit
By its own moods interprets, every where
Echo or mirror seeking of itself,
And makes a toy of Thought.

Coleridge seems to be suggesting it is only human to project onto this thing the inner moods of our idling Spirit. This was clearer in an earlier draft: 'To [the film] the living spirit in our frame, / that loves not to behold a lifeless thing, / transfuses its own pleasures, its own will'. But whereas the draft is open to Keats' criticism, the final version presents things without explaining them away. This task of poetry, to express delight and awe at the world as it is, and at the potential for *creatio ex nihilo*, often means contenting oneself with half-knowledge.

But should that be poetry's charge? Is such delight merely childish? How can we write of miracle and mystery in our scientific age? Late in the play Lear fancifully, perhaps half-madly, imagines life in prison with Cordelia as a sort of paradise:

No, no, no, no! Come, let's away to prison.
We two alone will sing like birds i' th' cage.
When thou dost ask me blessing, I'll kneel down
And ask of thee forgiveness. So we'll live,
And pray, and sing, and tell old tales, and laugh
At gilded butterflies, and hear poor rogues
Talk of court news; and we'll talk with them too-
Who loses and who wins; who's in, who's out-
And take upon 's the mystery of things,
As if we were God's spies;

I love those last lines: to take upon oneself the mystery of things. Importantly, it adds a dimension of responsibility to Keats' half-knowledge. The indefinite in Keats might be dismissed as a receptacle for one's own imagination and romantic fantasies. Like Leopardi's *siepe* it suggests the infinite, but it is an infinity onto which the poet is free to project himself. Lear's phrase suggests something more, a responsibility to care for and preserve the necessary place of mystery in the world, and of one's need to come to terms with the inexplicable, beginning with the miracle of one's own life. 'Thy life's a miracle' says the disguised Edgar to his father. Gloucester believes he has just jumped from the cliffs of Albion, so the grounds for Edgar's words are false. Gloucester's fall and survival is a deception. And yet there is no irony in what Edgar says. The truth of the affirmation remains. If anything it hits home more strongly to the audience because they see this double vision: the truth resting on a falsehood, but still as true as ever it can be in a world gone awry.

Edgar's sense of miracle is hard to hold on to. It is not the monotony of reality that dulls perception, but a lack of meaning. That lack can be like a veil that mutes the world, or it can steep us in a pessimism that Gloucester admirably expresses, 'we have seen the best of our time: machinations, hollowness, treachery and all ruinous disorders follow us disquietly to our graves'. It is this lack that Coleridge struggles against in 'This Lime-Tree Bower my Prison':

> . . . Hence forth I shall know
> That nature ne'er deserts the wise and pure;
> No plot so narrow, be but nature there,
> No waste so vacant, but may well employ
> Each faculty of sense, and keep the heart
> Awake to Love and Beauty!

It would be nice if these sentiments could stand as a manifesto against the difficulties of our age. But the rhetorical high pitch of Coleridge as he reaches the climax of the poem is hard to enjoy today. A calmer, clearer voice is wanted, one that doesn't mince words or let too much weight be born by those old traves, Love and Beauty. Perhaps a voice like Cordelia's. However stubborn she may appear in the play's first scene, and however naive it may be to rely on virtue and action to speak for her, Cordelia's dilemma is our own. What her sisters have just said leaves her without words and keenly aware of the enormous struggle she must undertake to speak with a skerrick of sincerity. She finds herself on a stage that has had its fair share of the empty rhetoric of playful dissimulation and self-aware deception.

\*

It is sometimes said by poets that translation is useful to fill in those moments when one feels there really is nothing to say. In translation one is never faced with the blank page because there is already something concrete to work with. In this sense translation puts a positive spin back on *ex nihilo nihil fit* and brings things back to Lucretius, for whom everything comes from pre-existing material. You could take it a step further and say all poems, not just their translations, arise out of pre-existing elements. The constituent atoms of a poem are the words of a language and its community of speakers. These existed before the poet, and in most cases will continue to do so long afterwards.

But translation is useful for poets for another reason too. As a check against the dangers accompanying the view of poetry I have been describing. Sometimes in the creative act hubris leads writers to think that they, god-like, must conjure a world out of nothing. They forget the relation of the created work to reality and to the community which gives it value; they forget the complex histories and values of the poem's words. Instead they seek a self-sufficient idiolect, a bastion against the instability and absurdity of the world. That of course is the paradox of language: a medium common to many and therefore impersonal, that one wants to personalize in order to express one's individuality. Cordelia knows this only too well. What words can she find to express herself after that assault on language by her sisters?

Translation is a reminder that writers do not pull rabbits out of a hat. They respond to an existing situation, and they take mystery on board. For just as a translator owes an allegiance to the original poem, so too the poet owes an allegiance to render reality. We can take this analogy a step further and say, just as reality is unstable and evades the author's attempts at representation, so too the original poem will always remain at one remove from the translator. Roman Jakobson gave the most theoretical weight to such ideas in the twentieth century in numerous essays including 'Linguistic Aspects of Translation' (1959), but of course poets have long been declaring just that. Dante says in the *Convivio* I, vii, 14, 'nulla cosa per legame musaico armonizzato si può della sua loquela in altra trasmutare sanza rompere tutta la sua dolcezza e armonia'.

The contemporary French poet Yves Bonnefoy has discussed such ideas at length. He is of the opinion that in translation, only creative transposition is possible. To argue this point Bonnefoy makes a distinction between an individual poem and Poetry as a force and an activity. The poem, in a sense, is not an end in itself, but rather a window onto something behind the writing of the poem and its language: an experience of the world. Bonnefoy names this catalyst the *acte*. The translator's task is to evoke that act again, that initial intention or intuition, in another language and cultural context.

In Bonnefoy's distinction between poem and Poetry lies both the impossibility and potential of translation. A poem is a unique language object that cannot be translated. But a poem is itself a searching after something beyond language, and thus Poetry can be translated. Where the translator is open to that initial experience, Poetry may take a new form in the translation. In framing the question of translation in this way Bonnefoy advocates the possibility of recreation, but also of fidelity to an initial spirit. Such a spirit remains vulnerable to criticisms that are not dissimilar to those that arise in discussions of Keats' half-knowledge and Leopardi's infinite, that is, that it is all too vague. Bonnefoy shirks such problems, and talks of the need for an affinity between poet and translator. He is motivated by a rigorous sense of responsibility to that which he translates. His own translations exemplify a lifelong engagement with the poem, the poet, and language. Or perhaps an obsession. I am reminded of Ezra Pound and his decades-long obsession with Cavalcanti. Pound tried all sorts of ways to bring Cavalcanti to life in the early twentieth century. He started by doing translations in Pre-Raphaelite Wardor Street English, but thirty years later he was translating some of the same poems in a pseudo-Elizabethan English in the belief it got closer to thirteenth-century Italian. He also wrote original poems in the voice of Cavalcanti, and then there are the essays, and finally the Opera (both the music and libretto) about the life of Cavalcanti. It was as if Pound were living between two worlds, his own and that of medieval Florence. But then I suspect that deep down most translators believe in metempsychosis.

What I want to focus on briefly is another aspect of this analogy between poet and translator. Like Pound, both writers and translators exist in a state of in-betweeness, or, as Simone Weil described, adopting a concept from Plato, in a state of *metaxy*. Between two languages and cultures; between the original and the rendition; between reality and the poem; between the creative act and nothingness; between our subjective selves and external reality. The role of go-between is rarely easy. Translators are familiar with that experience when, after having worked on the translation of a poem for some time, it becomes impossible to read that original without one's own version intruding. Suddenly, neither the original nor the translation exist independently of each other, and the translator is never wholly satisfied with either. Neither is an end in itself. One is caught between them.

Most of all the poet is caught in-between two conceptions of creation. On the one hand, poets are heroes who struggle to summon their poems out of the void, like a monotheistic god.

On the other hand, they align themselves with the view expressed by Lucretius in which poetry, like translation, arises out of the pre-existing atoms of the world. We may swing between these conceptions, but ultimately both of them require us to take Lear's mystery on board. Weil writes, 'The essence of created things is to be intermediaries. They are intermediaries leading from one to the other and there is no end to this. They are intermediaries leading to God. We have to experience them as such'. So that it is not far-fetched to consider translation (both as an activity and a state of mind) to be an analogy for writing and living in general. One is always in a state of metaxy. To adapt another aphorism of Weil's, poetry out of nothing (she talks of the material world as a whole) is a closed door. It is a barrier. And at the same time it is the way through.

## Works Cited

Dante Alighieri, *Convivio*, ed. C. Vasoli and D. De Robertis, Ricciardi, 1998.

Marcus Aurelius, *Meditations*, trans. Maxwell Staniworth, Penguin Classics, 2004.

Yves Bonnefoy, *Entretiens sur la poésie*, Mercure de France, 1992.

Samuel Taylor Coleridge, *Poetical Works*, Oxford University Press, 1912.

Roman Jakobson, 'On Linguistic Aspects of Translation.' in *The Translation Studies Reader*, ed. Lawrence Venuti, Routledge, 2004.

John Keats, *Letters of John Keats to his Family and Friends*, ed. Sidney Colvin, Macmillan,1925.

Lucretius, *On the Nature of Things*, trans. W. H. D. Rouse, revised Martin F. Smith, Loeb Classical Library, Harvard University Press, 1924.

William Shakespeare, *King Lear*, ed. Roma Gill, Oxford University Press, 2002.
Simone Weil, *La pesanteur et la grâce* (1947), trans. Emma Crawford, *Gravity and Grace*, Routledge, 1963.

# Cosmic Pessimism:
# On Leopardi

.....................................................

Giacomo Leopardi's *Canti*, or 'Songs', is one of the most influential works of nineteenth-century European literature. There are only forty-one of them, but they were the distillation of a lifetime's thinking in poetry, continually reworked until the author's death in 1837 at the age of thirty-nine. They include some of the most famous poems in Italian. Leopardi lived much of his life in Recanati, a backwater within the backward Papal States near Ancona. This spurred him on to become something of a literary prodigy: by eleven he had translated Horace's *Odes*, and was well on the way to having taught himself Greek, Hebrew, French, Spanish and English. His father had already dismissed the priest who was instructing young Giacomo in Latin for having nothing more to teach him. Through his teenage years he embarked on what he later described as 'seven years of insane and desperate study' in his father's library of sixteen-thousand volumes. He ruined his health and developed a serious hunchback.

Leopardi is Italy's great Romantic poet, and while there are similarities with Wordsworth and Coleridge, the contrasts are more striking. Most of these stem from Giacomo's cosmic pessimism. Nature, for example, is personified as a cruel wet-nurse, *dura nutrice*. Leopardi looked to classical authors for ideals of rationality and stoicism to face the suffering and nullity of the world. For this he was at odds with his century's frenzied rallying calls to nationalism and progress, and more in line with Schopenhauer and Nietzsche, both of whom he influenced. For the great literary historian Francesco De Sanctis, Leopardi's scepticism heralds the end of the world of theology and metaphysics and the inauguration of Modernity's material nihilism. Leopardi, like many later writers, turned to explore his own inner world, dominated as it was by unhappiness and pain. These could only be alleviated by self-illusion. If Gray coined the one-liner about childhood, 'ignorance is bliss', Leopardi turned it into a philosophical stance. Progress of the human spirit 'consists not in the discovery of positive truths, but of substantially negative ones'. These truths merely strip away the veils that make life bearable and spiritually rich. Science determines things, whereas it is the indeterminate that lets us breathe. 'How much greater the idea of the Antipodes was when Petrarch said that *perhaps* they exist, than as soon as it was known that they did', he writes. Like Wordsworth he thought childhood the happiest time in one's life.

If Leopardi remained childish, as poets are said to do, he was the child who never stopped asking why. He was never going to be happy hiding behind a hedge and imagining the horizon:

*Ma perché dare al sole,*
*Perché reggere in vita*
*Chi poi di quella consolar convenga?*
*Se la vita è sventura,*
*Perché da noi si dura?*

But why bring to light,
why educate
someone we'll console for living later?
If life is misery,
why do we bear it?

In the end he is closer to the Wordsworth of 'The Ruined Cottage' than the daffodils, or even the *Prelude*, for unlike Wordsworth he couldn't continue to celebrate and seek a union with nature once childhood's golden glow had vanished from the world.

Two criticisms of Leopardi are common. Firstly, he is a philosopher masquerading as a poet — what Croce dismissively called a mix of lyric description and philosophical argument, but Heidegger more favourably considered thinking in poetry. Secondly, he is too pessimistic. It is true that one of his favourite expressions is *invano*, in vain, and in a famous poem ruminating on lives destroyed like ants by nature's outpouring at Pompeii he mocks those who find means to praise:

*Venga colui che d'esaltar con lode*
*Il nostro stato ha in uso, e vegga quanto*
*É il gener nostro in cura*
*All'amante natura*

Let him who loves to praise our state
come to these slopes and see how well our kind
is served by loving nature.

Yet Leopardi in his best poems is a perfect example of that paradox of art that even where it makes us feel most strongly the unhappiness and nullity of things it can also be beautiful and uplifting.

Jonathan Galassi, who has previously translated Montale and Primo Levi, has done a fine job in re-presenting Leopardi to English-speakers. His notes glean from mountains of commentary and scholarship with a light touch and offer many of the delightful passages from the *Zibaldone*, the philosophical/poetical notebooks Leopardi kept throughout his life. His translations read fluidly, though I wonder whether this is always such a good thing. It comes at the cost of flattening out the linguistic flourishes of the Italian. These can sometimes be exasperating where Leopardi comes under the sway of the period's penchant for archaisms and syntactical acrobatics, but the startling contrast when we reach the simplicity of Leopardi's great idylls and elegies, which was to mark the beginning of so much of what came later in poetry, has also been smoothed over.

## Works Cited

Giacomo Leopardi, *Canti,* trans. Jonathan Galassi, Penguin Classics, 2010.

# The Big and the Little Prizes: On Thomas Bernhard

......................................................................

'Honored Minister, honored guests, there is nothing to praise, nothing to damn, nothing to accuse, but much that is absurd, indeed it is all absurd, when one thinks about death.' Thus began Thomas Bernhard's speech on the occasion of receiving the Austrian State Prize for Literature. The pomp and circumstance of such an event, along with the expectation that a recipient graciously praise jury, state, and the nation's literature, would sweep aside the contrariness of most writers. But not Bernhard, who throughout his career never swayed from reminding himself and many admiring readers that life really is absurd when one thinks about death.

Thomas Bernhard (1931–1989) was one of the most significant German-language writers of the second half of the twentieth-century. He was Austrian, but it was outside Austria that his novels and plays gained most favourable recognition. At home he was infamous as a *Nestbeschmutzer*, a nest-defiler, for his frequent bitter criticisms of Austrian society. *My Prizes* is no different in its attacks on his homeland, but what becomes clear is that Austria takes the brunt of a misanthropic nihilist's grudge against society at large:

> What we are speaking of here is unfathomable, we are not prop-
> erly alive, our existence and suppositions are all hypocritical . . .
> appearances are deadly and all the hundreds and thousands of
> hackneyed words we play with in our heads in our loneliness,
> . . . the words to which we cling because our impotence makes
> us insane and our insanity makes us despair, these words merely
> infect and ignore, blur and aggravate, shame and falsify and
> cloud and darken everything . . . '.

In the pieces that make up *My Prizes* Bernhard recounts events surrounding his acceptance of various literary awards, as well as providing some of the acceptance speeches. Bernhard the character displays the same impulsive, obsessive and uncompromising nature as the protagonists of his novels and plays. Prize money is at the centre of most of these pieces. If the inanity of awards and their ceremonies is a manifestation of the absurdity of social life as a whole, much of the angst and pleasure of these pieces derives from the way Bernhard, too, must play his part because he needs the cash. Caught in such a bind he rails against himself with characteristic vitriol. Take, for example the following passages from the awarding of the Austrian State Prize, an episode where Bernhard gets particularly worked up, because he had been awarded the Small Prize and not the Big Prize:

> Secretly I was thinking that the jury was indulging itself in sheer
> effrontery in giving me the Small Prize when of course the only
> thing I felt absolutely prepared to accept, should the question
> arise, and it had already been raised, was the Big Prize and not
> the Small, that it must be giving my enemies on this jury a

fiendish pleasure to knock me from my pedestal by throwing the Small Prize at my head.

It is hard to give a sense of Bernhard in a review, because the particularity of his prose is the way he or his characters get caught up in repetitive and ranting monologues that build magnificent pictures of obsessiveness. A few pages later he is still at it:

> When people asked me who had already won this so-called Big State Prize, I always said, All Assholes, and when they asked me the names of these assholes I listed a whole row of assholes for them and they'd never heard of any of them, the only person who knew of them was me. So this Cultural Senate, they said, is made up of nothing but assholes because you say that everyone in the Cultural Senate is an asshole. Yes, I said, the Cultural Senate is full of assholes, what's more they're Catholic and National Socialist assholes plus the occasional Jew for window dressing. I was repelled by these questions and these answers. . . . But I said I'd sworn to come to terms with this huge dirty trick. I'm not willing to give up twenty-five thousand schillings, I said, I'm greedy for money, I have no character, I'm a bastard too.

Once Bernhard receives the prize money, however, he is just as likely to throw it away impulsively, as if to balance out the reckless choice of juries. In two separate and very funny stories he recounts his impetuous acquisition first of a sports car, and then a dilapidated house in the country. This second purchase he could hardly see owing to thick fog on the inspection day, but he determined he had to have it then and there because the real estate agent kept describing the building's 'exceptional proportions': 'and the more often he asserted this, the clearer it became to me that he was right, in the end it wasn't *him* saying the property had exceptional proportions, it was *me* saying it, and saying it at every moment'.

Bernhard, one imagines, would have hated the expression 'life is a series of compromises'. Once he or his protagonists had determined that life was meaningless, there was no point stepping back from the abyss to make the best of things. In this, he fits into a tradition of the Nietzschean artist-hero who revels in his madness and uncompromising individuality. The results often make for exhilarating reading, perhaps because we take pleasure in his ability to give voice to our own secret outrages. But after a while such inveighing wears thin. One of the awards Bernhard discusses here is perhaps the most important German-language prize, the Georg Büchner. Ten years before Bernhard, this same honour had been bestowed on Paul Celan, a poet well aware of 'the majesty of the absurd which bespeaks the presence of human beings'. Yet his address on that occasion, the beautiful and now famous Meridian speech, was also able to give voice to the way 'art makes for distance from the I'. Like T. S. Eliot, Celan knew of that mysterious need to create and celebrate in the face of absurdity which was articulated in *Ash Wednesday*: 'Consequently I rejoice, having to construct something / Upon which to rejoice'. The contrast is telling. Bernhard has become a spoilt child still railing because the enchanting box of life he had been promised, and which was said to hold a world of delights, turned out to contain a little gift, not a big one.

## Works Cited

Thomas Bernhard, *My Prizes. An Accounting*, trans. Carol Brown Janeway. Alfred Knopf, 2010.

# The Pragmatic Idealist: On Machiavelli

Not many people have had an adjective describing a character trait coined from their name, even fewer one that has been widely used for over four hundred years. Yet almost immediately following publication of *The Prince* in England in 1584, *machiavellian* became a byword for cunning and unscrupulous pragmatism in politics. Already we find Shakespeare putting the following boast into the mouth of Richard III in *3 Henry VI*, 'I can add colours to the chameleon, / Change shapes with Proteus for advantages, / And set the murderous Machiavel to school'. In English the grimness of the adjective (early on often spelt *machiavillian*) was helped by its similarity to *villain*, but other languages felt just as strongly about the Florentine author: *machiavellico* in Italian, *machiavélique* in French, and *machiavellistisch* in German. So who was Niccolò Machiavelli and what exactly did he write that caused such an instant and enduring scandal throughout Europe?

In this new book Christopher Celenza, a professor in classics at John Hopkins University, aims to paint a portrait for the generalist reader through a discussion of his major texts, including *The Prince, The Discourses, and that delightful play The Mandragola*. Born in Florence in 1469, Machiavelli was trained in the *studia humanitatis*, those fundamental ingredients for the rebirth of culture we call the Renaissance: grammar, rhetoric, history, poetry and moral philosophy, all studied through the medium of Latin and its classical authors. It was thanks to this learning that Machiavelli, aged only 29, began his career as a Florentine ambassador: firstly at the French court, then with brutal dictator Cesare Borgia, and finally at the Papacy in Rome.

As Celenza reminds us, this was a turbulent political period. Unlike neighbouring France, Spain and the Hapsburg Empire to the north, all of which were under strong centralized governments, Italy was at best a geographical term for a collection of warring city states, now fiercely independent, now under the sway of powerful foreign alliances. Fortune's wheel turned fast and many were crushed as each new leader took the stage. These included a number of popes, whose earthly preoccupations might surprise us today. Julius II, for example, who features prominently in *The Prince*, lost no time, once elected, in forming an army to conquer Perugia and Bologna.

In 1512 Fortune also abandoned Machiavelli. Julius II had formed an alliance with the Spanish to drive the French out of Italy. The Florentine republic, a French ally, capitulated. The Medici family was reinstalled. Soon afterwards Machiavelli, accused of conspiring against the Medici, was imprisoned and tortured. On his release he was forced to live on his small estate outside of Florence, where, despite repeated attempts to return to an active political life, he would remain until his death in 1527 at the age of 58.

In exile Machiavelli turned to literary pursuits. As Celenza notes, 'few works command such fascination as *The Prince*'. Strange indeed then that it should take the genre, popular at the time, of advice manual for the successful ruler. Such guides tended to follow classical models and emphasise the need for *virtus*: a term taken from Roman moralists Cicero and Seneca to encompass wisdom, justice, courage, and temperance. Machiavelli's contemporaries coupled this idea with a Christian perspective which emphasised the spiritual dangers of allowing the ends to justify the means. Machiavelli's novelty was to state that if a ruler wishes to obtain his goals he will not always find it rational to be moral. One should certainly strive to be just, but one must also be willing to adapt one's behaviour to suit the winds of Fortune. If, as Machiavelli states, men are nothing but 'ungrateful, fickle feigners and dissemblers, avoiders of danger and eager for gain', then a successful ruler will sometimes need to be immoral. And on the question of the prince's accountability to God? Silence.

Celenza's discussion of *The Prince* gives the reader a fair overview of the major themes. Unfortunately it rarely carries Machiavelli out of the shadows of his work and into the realm of biography. A challenge for any biographer is to bring the cultural and political landscape of Renaissance Florence to life, but we hardly get beyond phrases such as, 'The world was fundamentally different then, and Machiavelli's gift was his ability to see that world as it was'. One suspects that in searching to write an accessible book Celenza has misjudged his audience. The result is a reminiscent of another political trait (one Machiavelli lacked), a capacity to speak without saying anything of substance.

Francis Bacon famously said, Machiavelli's only fault was 'to write what men do, not what they ought to do'. The irony is that while he was certainly a pragmatist there was also an idealistic streak to his character. In a famous letter he describes the role of his beloved classical authors:

> In the evening I return home and enter my study. At the door I take off my work clothes, covered in dust and dirt, and I put on clothing to appear before a king. And thus I enter the ancient courts of men who have long since died. There I am warmly welcomed, and I feed on the only food I find nourishing and was born to savour. I talk openly with them, and ask them to explain their actions, and they, out of kindness, respond. Four hours will easily pass by in this manner. I forget every worry. I am no longer afraid of poverty or frightened by death. I live entirely through them.

This vignette, so characteristic of Renaissance humanism, is hard to fit with Shakespeare's murderous Machiavel. Commenting on the above letter, Celenza writes, 'We sense a Machiavelli at home in different environments, who needs the give and take of vigorous human interaction'. That's poor nourishment indeed.

## Works Cited

Christopher S. Celenza, *Machiavelli A Portrait*, Harvard University Press, 2015.

# Seneca and the Art of Compromise

.......................................................................................

'To err is human, to persist in it is diabolical.' 'The greatest empire is to be emperor of oneself.' 'All life is nothing but a path to death.' These are a few of many memorable aphorisms by the Latin author Lucius Annaeus Seneca, known to the world as Seneca the Younger. What was it about writers of the classical world that encouraged them to speak as moral guides and to encapsulate life truths in pithy phrases? It seems so at odds with our own age, where more often than not literature privileges diversion and illusion. This leads to a second question. Why do we return so readily to ancient authors as sources of wisdom? If it's because we imagine the world they inhabited to have been simpler, one in which it was easier to invoke words like *truth*, then we're wrong. As this new biography by Emily Wilson makes clear, Seneca's world was far more chaotic, ruthless and precarious than our own. Seneca, who was born around 4 BCE, lived under three of the Roman empire's most notorious emperors, Caligula, Claudius and Nero. In his essay *On Anger* Seneca tells the story of a young man whose elegant clothes displeased Caligula. The emperor had him jailed and then, further enraged by the father's petition, executed. Caligula then invited the father to dinner, and set slaves to watch that he accepted everything he was offered and showed no sign of anger or sadness. 'You ask me why the father did this?' Seneca writes. 'Because he had another son.'

Under Caligula, and until he was in his forties, Seneca seems to have kept a low profile. Due to chronic illness he was slow to set out on the *cursus honorum*, the tenure track to power and glory which his father was ambitious to see his three sons undertake (Seneca's elder brother Novatus is mentioned in *Acts 18* where he was Roman magistrate responsible for dismissing charges brought against Paul). Everything changed in 41 CE when Seneca was exiled to Corsica by the new emperor Claudius. In exile his fame as an essayist and dramatist grew, such that eight years later he was recalled to Rome by the ambitious Agrippina to tutor her son Nero. When Nero became emperor aged seventeen it was Seneca who took on the role of his speechwriter and closest advisor. He remained Nero's right-hand man for the next eight years, through a period that saw the emperor murder his stepbrother and then his own mother. In the process Seneca amassed a huge fortune.

Seneca's wealth and closeness to Nero have long puzzled biographers. How does this fit with the stoic philosopher who wrote memorable one-liners like 'wealth is the slave of the wise man, the master of the fool'? Simply a case that it's easier to give than heed advice? Wilson does a good job of pointing out the importance of *dissimulatio*, or flattery and doublespeak, in Seneca's work. Rome was a society where survival depended on a complex set of networks, and exchanging of favours and obligations. If Seneca had one eye on future fame when he wrote, the other was firmly fixed on how his contemporary allies and enemies would interpret every word. It is also worth remembering that unlike our own proclivity to narrow in on personal experience, Seneca wrote outwards, after the general and universal. So that when he discusses wealth and exile we rarely get a reliable biographical perspective. This makes things difficult for the biographer, and the reader has to get used to phrases beginning 'it is just possible that . . .'.

Around 62 CE, now in his mid sixties, Seneca began to step back from public life. Nero had begun to favour other advisors and Seneca's star was on the wane, but any clear break or announcement of retirement would have been seen as betrayal. He had to tread carefully and hide behind his chronic lung condition. Future generations can be thankful that he did, because it was in his last years that Seneca produced his greatest work, the 124 letters to Lucilius. The letters are sophisticated rhetorical constructions, characterized by those memorable one-liners, by a snappy pace and wide-ranging illustrations from the life of contemporary Rome. These were the models for Montaigne's *Essays*, and it was these that made Seneca an example of pagan rectitude for church authors like Jerome. Indeed up until the Middle Ages it was thought Seneca was the author of a series of letters to St Paul, and it was claimed that he had converted to Christianity and was baptized by the bath of his death.

Death is the dominant theme of Seneca's letters. 'We die every day. You see, every day a little bit of our life is taken away from us, and even while we are growing our life is decaying'. In 65 CE Seneca was accused of involvement in a plot to assassinate Nero. He was ordered to commit suicide, thus fulfilling his own name according to some early biographers, since in Latin *se necans* means 'killing oneself'. His suicide in the bath was memorably depicted by Rubens, who shows stoicism and literature victorious over death. For Seneca Stoicism meant two things: public service and the private pursuit of wisdom and virtue. This fine biography reminds us just how hard it can be to pursue those goals simultaneously.

## Works Cited

Emily Wilson, *Seneca. A Life*, Allen Lane, 2015.

# The Firefly:
# On Pasolini

..................................

Pier Paolo Pasolini is best known to the English-speaking world
as auteur of such iconoclastic films of the sixties and seventies
as *The Gospel According to Matthew*, *La ricotta*, *Medea*, and *The
120 Days of Sodom* (and if we needed reminding, this new publication, *The Selected Poetry of Pier Paolo Pasolini*, comes with a
Foreword by James Ivory, whose foundation financed the project). But by the time Pasolini made his first film *Accattone* in
1961 he was already famous in Italy as a poet who had shaken up
the status quo of hermeticism's introspective and arcane lyrics,
and as the key neorealist novelist of his generation, whose first
novel had been put on trial for obscenity. Indeed one of the difficulties of talking about Pasolini, and the principal reason for
his continuing mystique, is the range of his genius, as Stephen
Sartarelli notes in a useful introduction. Was he a filmmaker
or poet? A traditional formalist or radical experimentalist? A
Marxist or a Catholic? Elitist aesthete or exhibitionist? Artist or
one-man political movement? Pasolini, who believed in the eternal coexistence of opposites, would probably have said, all of

the above. No figure embodies the polarized political situation and complex social tensions of Italy in this period so well. At the same time he is the most unique and narcissistic of artists. More than other mediums in which he worked his poetry manifests these contradictions. Here the inward-looking lyric urge wrestles with the desire to give voice to the demos — to become a civic poet in a tradition stretching back to Leopardi and Dante.

Published in 1957, *Gramsci's Ashes* first brought Pasolini's poetry to wider public attention and remains his most important volume. He termed these longish pieces *poemetti*, or mini epics, and their form resurrected Dante's *terza rima*. This shape allowed Pasolini to be both argumentative and take in gargantuan swathes of contemporary life, a fashion reminiscent of Allen Ginsberg. Pasolini's style in this period is one of contamination: baroque floridness interrupts prosaic sprawl, ideological expositions sit beside highly personal reflections, Shelley is invoked alongside Marx. Done well such plurilingualism is exhilarating. However it is resistant to translation (and hard to give indicative samples of here), and my only reservation with this otherwise fine edition is the flatter linguistic patina in English.

If the ideological regalia of these poems have dated, this is because there are now no alternatives to our all-pervasive liberal consumer society. But as Pasolini, whose vision grew increasingly pessimistic towards the end of his life, was at pains to point out, the demise of class diversity was accompanied by a much greater loss. The ancient belief systems sustaining Italy's agrarian society were suddenly vanishing. The traditions of the original Roman lower classes, who had been pushed to slums on the outskirts of the city under Mussolini, and which Pasolini celebrated in his early films and fiction, were now being replaced by a culture of amoral individualism. For poets such changes meant (and still mean) an erosion of the reality on which the symbols and myths of our society are nurtured. We lose a living connection with our cultural patrimony. In a famous essay concerning the vanishing fireflies from the Italian countryside Pasolini described this process with characteristic polemic as anthropological genocide.

As a testament to such issues and the heady political period in which he lived, however, I can't help feeling that his prose and films will be of more lasting value. Poetry and activism rarely sit well together. Auden, who famously said poetry makes nothing happen, was wary of *l'art engagé*. It may create that illusion of social relevance every artist hankers after, but the consequence is shallow roots and a tree that withers quickly. Who still remembers Wordsworth's sonnets in praise of capital punishment? In a different way Auden himself was a civic poet. For his work gave expression to our struggle to be individual and humane and reasonable. His poems may not incite direct action, but like the hermeticism of Montale, they are sites of resistance and voices of clarity in a time of uncertainty. Today we are overwhelmed by the language of marketing and the plurality of voices vying to communicate with us. But in the absence of wider common values in which to judge such voices morally and aesthetically, it is the most insistent and loudest that enter our consciousness like mantras. Our ability to engage critically is broken down and the content is of secondary importance to the slogan. I like to think the role of poetry in such a context is it is to create stanzas that are rooms of language. We visit these rooms to encounter ourselves, to feel grounded in reality, to dream, to hope.

At the end of the title poem from *Gramsci's Ashes* Pasolini describes his struggle to live with a conscious heart (*cuore cosciente*). In the best of his mature work this tension produced lasting poems such as 'The Cry of the Excavator' and 'Plea to my

Mother'. It is also found in the lyric poetry he wrote in a little known Friulian dialect at the beginning of his career, generously sampled in this edition.

Pasolini never shied away from polemic. He was subjected to thirty-three trials over the course of his life, all eventually resulting in acquittals. He received numerous death threats, was expelled from the Communist party, was loathed and lauded in turn by the Church. With his tragic and mysterious murder in November 1975 the world lost what Sartarelli rightly describes as a creative juggernaut, one of the great human and intellectual dramas of our time.

## Works Cited

Pier Paolo Pasolini, *The Selected Poetry of Pier Paolo Pasolini*, ed. and trans. Stephen Sartarelli, University of Chicago Press, 2014.

# The Civic Hermit:
# On Italo Calvino

One of Calvino's favourite descriptions of himself was as a hermit. The ideal situation for a writer, he wrote, is one of anonymity. 'Only when the author has no face is he able to develop authority as a writer, for then it is only his writings which exist.' In the end books 'represent the best of our conscience'. Time and again in this new book, *Letters 1941–1985* by Italo Calvino, which trace the life of one of Italy's most important novelists from his youth in San Remo during the war to his death in 1985, Calvino stresses the need to let texts breathe and speak for themselves. After all, these were the decades of a backlash against the personality cult of the author, symbolized by the figure of Calvino's friend Roland Barthes, whose essay 'Death of the Author' was published in 1967. In a letter written the same year, Calvino stated 'the starting point should be to regard the author as dead, . . . for the critic the author does not exist, only a certain number of writings exist'. For the twenty-odd years Calvino lived in Paris, that sense of isolation extended to the Italian he wrote in. 'Today in my family my wife speaks to me in the Spanish of Rio de la

Plata and my daughter in the French of Parisian school children: the language in which I write no longer has anything to do with any spoken language, other than through my memory.'

Why do we turn to a writer's letters? Surely one reason is to follow authors' everyday endeavour to be true to themselves without betraying 'the human commitments that every action, every relationship with others involves'. Letters are symbolically so important in this struggle because they evoke a real person as interlocutor and are signed yours sincerely. But how might that work in the case of a self-confessed recluse? Do Calvino's letters need to be published? It is important to state that he was not an Italian J. D. Salinger. Calvino's correspondence is vast and varied and reveals he took his role as public intellectual very seriously. We see him as an editor for the important publishing house Einaudi in Turin, busy communicating with authors like Pasolini, Pavese and Sciascia. We see his involvement in, and 1957 resignation from, the Italian Communist Party. We see him as a writer for some of the important national dailies, including *La Repubblica*, founded by childhood friend Eugenio Scalfari, at a time when newspapers published opinion pieces by intellectuals and writers on a daily basis.

What we don't see, in part as a result of the editor's selections, is the private side of that struggle. This makes for an unbalanced picture. And balance was a central question for Calvino. As Cosimo, his hero of *The Baron in the Trees*, discovered, the decision to live in trees without ever touching the ground doesn't preclude the need to participate in society. Calvino says of Cosimo,

> I wanted to put forward the figure of a committed man (an intellectual, if you like), who takes a profound part in history and the development of society, but who knows he has to travel

different roads, as is the destiny of those who do not conform. I also wanted to express a moral imperative of will, of loyalty to oneself, to the law one has imposed on oneself, even when this costs us separation from the rest of mankind. Is this a credo of individualism? I would say that it is the affirmation that in order to be genuinely with others one must not be afraid to find oneself even on one's own.

It's all a question of finding the right distance in order to be both present and detached. The Polish poet Czesław Miłosz talked of something similar: the need for a poem to have the vast vision of a landscape seen from the air, and simultaneously the ability to home in on the twitch of a rabbit's ear.

Finding that perspective was not easy for Italian writers in the ideologically charged decades after the war. In a letter to Pasolini Calvino criticises the desire for topicality. It may give one a great sensation of being alive, 'but this is life in the world of effects, not in the world of slow reasoning and reflection'. In contrast he boasts of spending twelve hours a day reading. Yet six months earlier we read, 'in recent years I was very satisfied playing the dead man . . . whereas now I am starting again to realize that the one thing I would like is to write, publish, communicate'.

Calvino once wrote 'I have spent more time with other people's books than with my own'. It is tempting to hear only the tone of regret in this statement, but for a writer who believed in the social value of literature it would be strange if it were otherwise. Sometimes it seems that our existence is only given meaning through the quest to live our lives to the full, and that this fullness is measured through the self-gratification and the self-sufficiency of our subjectivities. None was more aware of this danger than Calvino, whose desire for solitude was checked by a belief that 'the right to exist needs to be earned and justified through that which we give to others'. In later letters he wrote less optimistically of society, 'my position today is probably to be found in that frightening core of desperation caused by the unliveable nature of the contemporary world and of the impossibility of active participation, because all roads to a desirable future are closed off'. And yet this self-confessed hermit continued to throw his creative energies into literature and communicate with a frankness and sincerity that still gives much courage to his readers.

## Works Cited

Italo Calvino, *Letters 1941–1985*, selected and with an introduction by Michael Wood, trans. Martin McLaughlin, Princeton University Press, 2013.

# Gathered by Ear:
# On Robert Frost

In one of his more memorable epigrams Robert Frost described poetry as 'a momentary stay against confusion', a heartening definition for budding poets if we consider the intensity of babble around us today. To remove some of the confusion surrounding Frost himself is among the editors' aims in this first of four planned volumes of his complete letters, *The Letters of Robert Frost Volume I 1886–1920*. It continues the commendable project by Harvard University Press of bringing into print all the primary material of one of America's most important twentieth-century poets. The popularity of Frost has not always been on the rise however. His death in 1963 coincided with the advancement of a fresh crowd who liked to dismiss the gruff New England farmer as an arch-formalist fit for the home truths of country almanacs. Things only got worse with the publication of the authorized biography and selected letters at the hands of Lawrance Thompson. Thompson successfully established his own fame by depicting his former friend as a brute, such that Helen Vendler in 1970 notoriously called Frost a 'monster of egotism' who left 'a wake of destroyed human lives'. So will these collected letters rebalance our picture? Judging by this first volume, which takes us up to Frost at age forty-six, he comes across very well; sympathetic, funny, self-deprecating, and both loyal and caring towards family and friends.

The first and shortest chapter here is entitled 'The Early Years', somewhat of a misnomer given that it covers the period up to his thirty-eighth year. But that's the thing with Frost. His literary career only began in 1915 when as an unknown and practically unpublished poet, with wife and four children, he borrowed money to travel to London in the hope of living by his writing in the literary capital of the world. He carried with him the man-uscripts of what would become his first two volumes of poetry, *A Boy's Will* and *North of Boston*. The two years that Frost spent in England were heady days. With the First World War looming, Frost found himself in the city that was gathering many of the names that would come to define the first wave of Modernism. In letters from this period we find him gate-crashing a party at Harold Monro's new Poetry Bookshop. He gets to know Yeats, whose manner 'is like that of a man in some dream he can't shake off. It is not a pose with him. He has to take himself that way.' And he falls in with that fascinating charlatan and arriviste Ezra Pound, for whom it was all a question of pose: he is 'six inches taller for his hair and hides his lower jaw in a delicate gold filigree of almost masculine beard. His coat is of heavy black velvet. He lives in Grub Street, rich one day and poor the next. His friends are duchesses. And he swears like a pirate.' Although Frost soon drifted away from this circle, Pound's name continues to appear in letters as a symbol of everything he wants to define himself against. 'I want to be a poet for all sorts and kinds. I could never make a merit of being caviar to the crowd the way my quasi-friend Pound does.'

In the early days of modernism it seems everyone had a manifesto or slogan to foist upon the world. Pound's 'make it new' is possibly the most bombastic of them all, but Frost was not immune to this disease. Letters show him formulating his theory of the auditory imagination. Rather than taking the sentence as just a grammatical cluster, Frost wanted to focus on the sound a sentence has. The way you get a feel for sense from the intonations of muffled voices heard through a door. Somewhat limited as a theory of poetry perhaps, but perfectly reasonable. Less so when he insists the human brain has an innate range of cadences similar to those of birds. Later he came to describe things more sensibly: 'there are the very regular pre-established accent and measure of blank verse; and there are the very irregular accent and measure of speaking intonation. I am never more pleased than when I get them into strained relation.'

Speaking intonations and colloquial language are what Frost consistently championed. If poets can be divided into those who, like Wordsworth, invoke the real language of men, and those like Mallarmé who seek the caviar, then Frost is clearly in the first group. A danger for this first type of writer is the tone of self-righteousness that creeps in when we assume the vernacular will grant tout court authenticity on a poem. This is untrue. However, it is also incorrect to accuse writers in the second group of abstraction. All language is abstract. The real problem is that words require constant attention to stop them drifting even further from reality through imprecise use. While few of us can cast the first stone here, most guilty are those for whom language is a tool to bully public opinion, or to beguile reality and one's own sentiments. Cutting through the weasel words of politicians and the poeticisms of lazy imaginations is the Sisyphean task poets of each age face. Shakespeare was one of our best clarifiers of the language, and it's pleasing to learn that Frost relished quoting the bard in his letters. As two brief examples will show, the lines he preferred aren't found in the speeches of Polonius: from *As You Like It*, 'Very good orators, when they are out, they will spit'; and from *Twelfth Night*, 'Aw, go shake your ears!'. Frost himself liked to advise people 'gather your sentences by ear'.

## Works Cited

*The Letters of Robert Frost Volume I 1886–1920*, ed. Donald Sheehy, Mark Richardson and Robert Faggen, Harvard University Press, 2014.

# Dante on the Run

Surely of all the great writers Dante is least in need of a biography. After all, in both *The Divine Comedy* and the *Vita Nuova* the main character, who is on a quest for intellectual and spiritual growth, appears to be the author himself. And yet, while on some level one may read the *Comedy* as a portent of Wordsworth's *Prelude*, which was subtitled 'Growth of a Poet's Mind', in other ways it is very different. We learn little of Dante's quotidian existence by reading his work. In medieval literature the writer was reluctant to discuss his personal life unless doing so served a useful purpose to others. Furthermore, our ideas of utility are radically different. For example, our own age considers childhood a formative period, but in Dante and his contemporaries it's rarely mentioned. From the very first line of the *Comedy*, 'Nel mezzo del cammin di nostra vita', the use of the plural pronoun 'we' presents Dante the character as an everyman, despite his self-proclaimed poetic genius which has entitled him to such a rare vision of the afterlife.

DANTE ON THE RUN

This biography by Marco Santagata, professor of Italian literature at the University of Pisa, is the latest of many such works that have attempted to uncover the real, or what medieval culture might have called the mundane Dante. At the outset I was sceptical. Italian scholarly language is not renowned for accommodating the general reader, and the genre of biography has thrived less in Italy than in the English-speaking world. Thankfully Santagata has written a book that translates well for an English audience. It is lively and a pleasure to read. Santagata's second career as a novelist may play a part here. Indeed the subtitle of the Italian version is 'Il romanzo della sua vita', which can be interpreted as 'his life as a novel', a description that might helpfully be applied to many biographies of Shakespeare. As with Shakespeare, our knowledge of the facts surrounding Dante is limited. Piecing them together requires a good deal of guesswork. Santagata does an excellent job highlighting the facts we do have, and setting out his arguments clearly whenever he enters the dark woods of supposition. There are over 100 pages of notes.

Of course as Dante's first biographer, Giovanni Boccaccio, realized, there is much that is larger than life in Dante's story. It should be a novel. Think of the outline: falling in love at age nine with Beatrice, a woman to whom he only spoke once or twice, yet whom he venerated all his life; sending his best friend Guido Cavalcanti into exile, and soon after treading that same path as political factionalism destroyed his beloved Florence; doggedly believing that Italian could be a literary language to rival Latin; writing one of the masterpieces of world literature while homeless and under a death sentence.

I must confess that I had always imagined exile to have been good for Dante's literary career. I pictured him stepping back from the chaos of his contemporary surroundings like the souls in heaven looking down on that threshing floor of earthly life, a hermit with his books and writings materials. Santagata paints a dramatically different scene. We see a man with no fixed income, worried about that death sentence, dependent on the generosity of patrons who are themselves caught up in political turmoil. Dante is shown first scheming with White comrades to regain Florence, then currying favour with Black factions to be forgiven and allowed home, then switching allegiances to become a fervent Ghibelline. It is amazing to me that he was able to concentrate enough to a write a sonnet let alone the 14,233 lines of the *Comedy*.

To chart Dante's movements after exile Santagata relies as he must on 'circumstantial reconstructions'. His argument, simplified here, is that the *Comedy* is full of political and social gossip, the equivalent of today's political memoir, a genre for which Italians have invented an English term, the 'Instant Book'. (Another example is the word 'footing', which Italians use to describe what we call 'jogging'). Because Dante writes on the run, or while footing, the decision regarding whom to damn is based on political expediency and reflects the author's changing allegiances over time, as if he were a Machiavellian avant la lettre. This is an interesting thesis, but I have two perplexities. The instant book is written for an instant audience — its effectiveness depends on reaching a wide public immediately. When we say the first part of the *Comedy*, *Inferno*, was published probably in 1314, we don't know what that means. How many manuscripts were made, how were they circulated? Certainly within a couple of decades of Dante's death in 1324 the poem was widely known. But if he wrote to influence his fortunes with his contemporaries that's another story. Secondly, the instant book tends to die an instant death as the news cycle moves on. What turned the *Comedy* from a collection of gossip into a masterpiece?

To be fair this last question was not part of Santagata's brief, and as the *Comedy* has fascinated scholars and readers for 700 years, it would be unreasonable to expect an instant answer. Still, it does remind us of the limits of relying too heavily on such a thesis. At the beginning of *De monarchia* Dante takes up an image found in *Psalms* of a tree flourishing along the banks of a river, and links it to the classical topos of desire for knowledge. But he then talks about the responsibility that tree has to bear fruit and transmit the knowledge it has been nourished on to future generations. I love that image. It is so characteristic of Dante's long vision, yoking classical and Christian traditions while stretching its sight into the future. Robert Gray in his poem 'To a Friend' says, 'In writing, it wasn't renown I was after; / it seemed instead an offering to one's ancestors'. Dante reminds us that poems are both offerings to our ancestors and prayers for our children.

## Works Cited

Robert Gray, *Cumulus. Collected Poems*, John Leonard Press, 2012.

Marco Santagata, *Dante. The Story of his Life*, trans. from the Italian by Richard Dixon, Harvard University Press, 2016.

# Squaring the Circle: Dante, Memory and the Project of Writing

Contrary to Plato's notion of the poet as a verbal magician who is unscrupulous with the truth, the poetry I admire and the poetry I try to write is very conscious of that nebulous ideal, truthfulness, and is motivated by the desire to know oneself. We write in order to understand our place in the world, to embody and order experiences in such a way that they resonate beyond the finite ego, to connect to a tradition, and to keep the language vital. In all of these aims one might detect a desire to gain a little control over our surroundings, whose complexity and fluidity never cease to amaze us. Without a sense of our continuity across time we have no identity, and thus part of our impetus to write is a desire to slow time down, and hold the past to us.

We can't underestimate the importance of memory for anchoring us in time. Yet we frequently portray memory as unstable. It is striking that the act of remembering, which is a function of our brains, is often depicted as a force external to ourselves. Perhaps this is indicative of our continuing poor understanding of how memory works, and our seeming lack of control over its operations. If memory is as messy and fluid as life itself, then it also comes under the sway of our desire to order and control it. Cicero stated in *De oratore* that 'order is what most brings light to our memory'. No wonder then that memory has long been tangled up with the act of writing, something confirmed by the figure of Mnemosyne, the classical personification of memory and mother of the nine Muses. In this essay I would like to reflect on the links between memory, the Muses and the act of writing by examining *Paradiso 33*, the final canto of Dante's *Commedia*. Of course as a field of investigation memory is a vast topic, and has been tackled fruitfully in disciplines as varied as psychology, biology, philosophy, linguistics and the arts. My purpose here is to focus on medieval conceptions of memory, particularly as they are presented in the work of Dante. I do so from the perspective of a poet. I hope to show that the link between memory and the impetus to write is profound and complex.

To talk of memory, Dante regularly makes use of two metaphors. The first conceives of memory as a book which conserves the past. The image is famously used at the beginning of his autobiographical work, *Vita Nuova*, where he writes, *In quella parte del libro de la mia memoria dinanzi a la quale poco si potrebbe leggere* (In that part of the book of my memory previous to which very little can be read). The second type of metaphor for memory is that of the stamp that impresses the past on the mind as if it were a surface of wax. In *Purgatorio 33 79–81* he writes:

*Sì come cera da suggello,*
*che la figura impressa non trasmuta,*
*segnato è or da voi lo mio cervello.*

Even as wax the seal's impressed,
where there's no alteration in the form,

113

so does my brain now bear what you have stamped.
(translations by Allen Mandelbaum)

Both metaphors link memory to the idea of representation, and thus also to that of interpretation: memory as a container or thesaurus, on the one hand, and on the other, memory as a stamp or a mark or an inscription, or a picture retained on a receptive surface. Both metaphors suggest an active storing and ordering process, akin to that of writing itself. For Dante and his contemporaries memory was not merely a receptacle for information, but a living faculty that required training and active use. It would have been inconceivable to say, as we so often do today, 'I'm sorry, my memory is no good — could you remind me of your name?' To the medieval mind the fault lay not with one's memory, but rather with one's inability to use this precious faculty well and keep it in good shape. These two metaphors for memory can be traced back to classical literature, and were still common beyond the Renaissance, as Mary Carruthers carefully detailed in her work *The Book of Memory*. The two conceptions are not mutually exclusive and often overlap. When Hamlet describes his memory first as a 'table' from which trivial matter can be wiped away, and then as 'the book and volume of my brain' where important matters are preserved, the two topoi combine — memory as graphic representation, and as a collection bound into a volume and kept safe, and presumably available to recall to those who understand its organisation. It is tempting to see in Hamlet's speech a two-fold process of writing: first drafting, then ordering and setting in place. Carruthers reminds us of the importance of distinguishing between the storing process and the process of recollection. If storing is equivalent to writing in a book, recollection is also an active process. It is itself a sort of composition, in which existing material is arranged in accordance with the here and now. Both activities might be considered prototypes for creative writing.

Reference to memory and invocations to the Muses are linked in the opening cantos of each of the three canticles of Dante's *Commedia*: *Inferno*, *Purgatorio*, and *Paradiso*. However, it is in the final canto of the entire work, *Paradiso* 33, that Dante explores the link between memory and writing in most detail. I would like to examine this canto. After a prayer by San Bernard to the Virgin Mary, Canto 33 is dedicated to a description of Dante *personaggio*'s final vision. The premise of the entire *Commedia* is that Dante the character, having undertaken a journey through the afterworld, sits down in a moment of Wordsworthian tranquillity to record his vision. In Canto 33 this act of recollection and writing reaches its climax. The last vision had been experienced by Dante the character as a glimpse of the overarching unity and harmony of the universe. As a vision, however, it remained just beyond the province of human comprehension. How can such a vision be recounted? What language, what poetry can do it justice? The canto is infused with a dramatic tension which derives from the movement backwards and forwards between the vision as it was first experienced and as it is felt and remembered in hindsight, and the moment of writing dominated by a feeling of inadequacy. Thus, the opening description of the vision is as follows:

> *E io ch'al fine di tutt' i disii*
> *approprinquava, sì com' io dovea,*
> *l'ardor del desiderio in me finii.*
> *Bernardo m'accenava, e sorridea,*
> *perch'io guardassi suso; ma io era*
> *già per me stesso tal qual ei volea:*

*ché la mia vista, venendo sincera,*
*e più e più intrava per lo raggio*
*de l'alta luce che da sé è vera.*

And I, who now was nearing him who is
the end of all desires, as I ought,
lifted my longing to its ardent limit.
Bernard was signalling — he smiled — to me
To turn my eyes on high; but I, already
was doing what he wanted me to do,
because my sight, becoming pure, was able
to penetrate the ray of light more deeply -
that light, sublime, which in itself is true. (Canto 33, 46–54)

This is immediately followed by the first passage describing the
difficulty of transcribing the experience of the vision. There
is a double difficulty: firstly, the inadequacy of language; and
secondly, the inadequacy of memory itself. In a famous simile
memory is compared to a dream — what remains from both, is
not a concrete object or event, but a sensation:

*Da quinci innanzi il mio veder fu maggio*
*che 'l parlar mostra, ch'a tal vista cede,*
*e cede la memoria a tanto oltraggio.*
*Qual è colui che sognando vede,*
*che dopo 'l sogno la passione impressa*
*rimane, e l'altro a la mente non riede,*
*cotal son io, ché quasi tutta cessa*
*mia visione, e ancor mi distilla*
*nel core il dolce che nacque da essa.*
*Così la neve al sol si disigilla;*
*così al vento ne le foglie levi*
*si perdea la sentenza di Sibilla.*

From that point on, what I could see was greater
than speech can show: at such a sight, it fails —
and memory fails when faced with such excess.
As one who sees within a dream, and, later,
the passion that had been imprinted stays,
but nothing of the rest returns to mind,
such am I, for my vision almost fades
completely, yet it still distils within
my heart the sweetness that was born of it.
So is the snow, beneath the sun, unsealed;
and so, on the light leaves, beneath the wind
the oracles the Sibyl wrote were lost. (Canto 33, 55–66)

It is the ephemeral nature of this sensation coupled with its sweetness that spurs the poet on to record the vision despite the impossibility of doing so. The verb *record* has at its origin the idea of recalling in memory, but memory housed not exclusively in the head, but also the heart, as the line *'nel core il dolce che nacque da essa'* reminds us.

What remains of the vision in the heart drips drop by drop, *distilla*, like a precious liquid. In a striking tercet this idea of a drop returns in the single moment, *un punto*:

*Un punto solo m'è maggior letargo*
*che venticinque secoli a la 'mpresa*
*che fé Nettuno ammirar l'ombra d'Argo.*

That one moment brings more forgetfulness to me than twenty-
five centuries have brought to the endeavor
that startled Neptune with the Argo's shadow. (Canto 33, 94–96)

One single moment of the vision, as now recovered drop by drop in the heart, comports more forgetfulness than the 25 centuries that have passed since Jason undertook his journey in the Argus. While this analogy emphasises the grandness of what lies beyond Dante's vision when compared to human affairs, it simultaneously affirms the power of memory aided by literature to stretch back 25 centuries and make connections with the past. And not just any past, but a key moment when the god Neptune first marvelled at the ingenuity of human kind, who had learnt to build a boat. Are we to see in Dante a similar ingenuity in recording his vision? In another famous simile Dante seems to suggest so.

In searching for a metaphor for his vision of the profound unity of the universe, he turns to the book:

*Nel suo profondo vidi che s'interna,*
*legato con amore in un volume,*
*ciò che per l'universo si squaderna:*
*sustanze e accidenti e lor costume*
*quasi conflati insieme, per tal modo*
*che ciò ch'i' dico è un semplice lume.*

In its profundity I saw — ingathered
and bound by love into one single volume —
what, in the universe, seems separate, scattered:
substances, accidents, and dispositions
as if conjoined — in such a way that what
I tells is only rudimentary. (Canto 33, 85–90)

The perfection of this unity, but also its unfathomableness, lies in that combination of the numbers three and four contained in the words *interna* and *quaderna*. The unifying of three and four, returns later in the canto in a geometrical simile which may at first seem out of place, that of squaring the circle:

*Qual è 'l geometra che tutto s'affige*
*per misurar lo cerchio, e non ritrova,*
*pensando, quel principio ond' elli indige,*

As the geometer intently seeks
to square the circle, but he cannot reach,
through thought on thought, the principle he needs (Canto 33,
133–135)

But in writing his vision Dante is doing something equally difficult, as the metaphor of the book reminds us. It is not enough for the vision to be evoked again. For Dante, remembrance must be an active process, rather than a passive and unexpected uprising like Proust's *madeleine*. If, as Plato states in *Menone*, to know something is to reawaken it in the memory, then the metaphor of the book takes on a further significance. The book suggests the idea of an ordering of past experience, and secondly preserving it in a structured form. Earlier in *Paradiso* Beatrice tells Dante:

*Apri la mente a quel ch'io ti paleso*
*e fermalvi entro; ché non fa scienza,*
*sanza lo ritenere, avere inteso.*

Open your mind to what I shall disclose,
and hold it fast within you; he who hears,
but does not hold what he has heard, learns nothing. (Canto
5, 40–42)

That is, open your mind to what I now reveal, and cherish it there, for comprehension alone, without preserving what is known, is nothing. That preservation of the past, *ritenere*, finds expression in the metaphor of the book, and is manifested in the process of writing.

The play on the numbers three and four in the passage just examined reminds us that the book of memory Dante is writing is a work of poetry. The *terza rima* in which the poem is composed requires the poet-rememberer to add a further level of complexity to the ordering system. In the context of medieval concepts of memory this should not merely be considered an ornamental sign of bravura on the part of the poet. For Dante, in keeping with the idea quoted in Cicero at the beginning of this essay, the rigorous nature of the ordering sheds light on memory, and is more likely to result in an accurate retrieval of the past when it is recollected. Add to this the mnemonic function of rhyme and metre, and the choice of *terza rima* (whose tri-part structure evokes that universal order of the trinity), and it becomes clear that the links between poetry and memory can be complex and deeply meaningful. To pay homage to memory and her nine daughters at the beginning of each canticle is so important to Dante because they literally are the stimulus to poetry.

By extension we might say that our cultural memory and knowledge need to be kept alive through actively returning to and interpreting the past. Seneca when talking of memory makes a similar distinction between the active and passive use of verbs like *recall*. It is a distinction between remembering and knowing, as he states in Epistle 33:

*Meminisse est rem commissam memoriae custodire. At contra scire est et sua facere quaeque nec ad exemplar pendere et totiens respicere ad magistrum.*

To remember is one thing, to know another. Remembering is merely overseeing a thing deposited in the memory; knowing is making the thing your own.

This desire to command the past through writing is, as I have suggested, a topos of classical literature. However, there is another important influence for Dante's concept of memory. In Augustine the soul is comprised of three parts, and thus it is a sign of the trinity in human nature: *memoria, intelligentia, voluntas*. Of these memory is considered the highest, and Augustine dedicates much of Book X of *The Confessions* to understanding it:

*Magna vis est memoriae, nescio quid horrendum, deus meus, profunda et infinita multiplicitas. et hoc animus est, et hoc ego ipse sum. quid ergo sum, deus meus? quae natura sum? varia, multimoda vita et immensa vehementer. ecce in memoriae meae campis et antris et cavernis innumerabilibus atque innumerabiliter plenis innumerabilium rerum generibus, sive per imagines, sicut omnium corporum, sive per praesentiam, sicut artium, sive per nescio quas notiones vel notationes, sicut affectionum animi (quas et cum animus non patitur, memoria tenet, cum in animo sit quidquid est in memoria), per haec omnia discurro et volito hac illac, penetro etiam quantum possum, et finis nusquam. tanta vis est memoriae, tanta vitae vis est in homine vivente mortalier.* (Book X, 17)

O my God, what a powerful force memory is, something awe-inspiring, a deep and boundless complexity. And this is the mind, and this is what I am. And what is that, my God? What kind of nature am I? A complex and manifold life and one that is utterly incalculable. Look. In the fields and caves and hollows of my memory (which are countless, and teeming with countless things of countless kinds), whether by means of impressions (as of every kind of physical object) or of things actually present (such as everything which has been learned) or through ideas and perceptions (such as emotions, which the memory preserves even when the mind is not experiencing them, since whatever is in the memory is in the mind): I crisscross between them and flit from one thing to another, I go as deep as I can, and I find there are no limits. That is how powerful a force memory is, a powerful life force in every living being born to die.

Memory is as vast and manifold as the world itself. In describing the numberless fields, caves and caverns that comprise memory, Augustine creates an impression of a universe beyond the control of the individual subject. While he runs and flies through this realm he finds that 'nowhere is there an end'. He seeks to know in which chamber of memory God might be located:

> *Ecce quantum spatiatus sum in memoria nea quaerens te, domine, et non te inveni extra eam. neque enim aliquid de te inveni quod non meminissem, ex quo didici te, nam ex quo didici te non sum oblitus tui. ubi enim inveni veritatem, ibi inveni deum meum, ipsam veritatem, quam ex quo didici non sum oblitus. itaque ex quo te didici, manes in memoria mea . . . Sed ubi manes in memoria mea, domine, ubi illic manes? quale cubile fabricasti tibi? quale sanctuarium aedificasti tibi? tu dignationem memoriae meae, ut maneas in ea, sed in qua eius parte maneas, hoc considero. . . .*
> (Book X, 24–25)

Look how widely I have ranged in my memory, Lord, in search of you. But I did not find you outside it. Nor have I found anything about you which I did not keep in mind from the time when I learned about you; for from the time when I learned about you I have not forgotten you. Where I found truth, there I found my God, Truth himself, truth which from the moment I learned of it, I did not forget. And so from the moment I learned of you, there you remain in my memory . . . Where do you abide in my memory, Lord, where in that place do you abide? What kind of resting place have you fashioned for yourself? What kind of sanctuary have you built for yourself? You have done my memory the honor of abiding in it: but I am now going to examine your precise location there.

Augustine examines his mind, but finally decides God cannot be located in any specific place. It is interesting that in Chapter X of *The Confessions*, with its extended analysis of memory, the metaphor of the book is not used. Only Borges' infinite library would do justice to Augustine's description here. Indeed, the endless searching that Augustine describes, and the sense of dizziness that comes from feeling overwhelmed by the vastness of memory and the inability to pin the deity down, is in contrast to God's imagined sanctuary. Memory, in both its power and limitations to deal with time and experience, is part and parcel of the human condition.

By contrast, Dante, in Canto 29 of *Paradiso*, states that angels have no need of memory. In their direct vision of God they are fully satisfied. Memory is redundant for those who have continuous and uninterrupted understanding:

*Queste sustanze, poi che fur gioconde*
*de la faccia di Dio, non volser viso*
*da essa, da cui nulla si nasconde:*
*però non hanno vedere interciso*
*da novo obietto, e però non bisogna*
*rememorar per concetto diviso.*

These beings, since they first were gladdened by
the face of God, from which no thing is hidden,
have never turned their vision from that face,
so that their sight is never intercepted
by a new object, and they have no need
to recollect an interrupted concept. (Canto 29 76–81)

For humans, consciousness is a continual stream of impressions each replacing the previous and impossible to hold. Angels, on the other hand, are constantly in touch with the source of that stream. In heaven there is a sort of dynamic stasis, which might be considered that sanctuary Augustine evokes with longing in *The Confessions*.

Returning to the final canto of *Paradiso* we find a similar idea. Dante's concluding vision of God transcends all human faculties, both mnemonic and expressive, in a way that recalls Augustine:

> *Da quinci inanzi il mio veder fu maggio*
> *che 'l parlar mostra, ch'a tal vista cede,*
> *e cede la memoria a tanto oltraggio.*

> From that point on, what I could see was greater
> than speech can show: at such a sight, it fails -
> and memory fails when faced with such excess. (Canto 33, 55–57)

The noun *oltraggio*, excess, of course contains none of its more recent negative connotations, but means that which is beyond all limits. Similarly, in the opening Canto of *Paradiso* Dante had confessed such limits:

> *Veramente quant'io del regno santo*
> *ne la mia mente potei far tesoro,*
> *sarà ora matera del mio canto.*

> Nevertheless, as much as I, within
> my mind, could treasure of the holy kingdom
> shall now become the matter of my song. (Canto 1,10–12)

This passage reaffirms the link between the metaphors of the book and treasure chest. Dante's description of his final vision may not reveal the deity to us, but in the dramatic oscillation between original vision, memory, and the act of writing, Canto 33 provides a fitting culmination to this extraordinary journey.

## Works Cited

Dante Alighieri, *La Vita Nuova*, in D. De Robertis (ed.), *Opere minori*, Ricciardi, 1984.

Dante Alighieri, *Commedia*, ed. G. Petrocchi, Le Lettere, 1994.

Dante Alighieri, *The Divine Comedy*, trans. A. Mandelbaum, Everyman Classics, 1995.

Augustine, *Confessions*, ed. and trans. C. J. B. Hammond, Harvard University Press, 2016.

M. Carruthers, *The Book of Memory: a Study in Memory and Medieval Culture*, Cambridge University Press, 2005.

Seneca, *Epistles*, Vol. 1, trans. R. Gunmere, Harvard University Press, 1917.

# New Wings of the House:
# On Lesbia Harford

Recognition can be a long time coming. Lesbia Harford, who died in 1927 at the age of thirty-six, is one of our best poets, but she was virtually unknown until 1985 when the first meaningful sample of her work appeared. That volume, edited by Drusilla Modjeska and Marjorie Pizer, was invaluable for creating awareness of Harford's poetry. But according to the editor of this new edition, Oliver Dennis, the insistence on presenting Harford as an activist and feminist poet in that 1985 selection has limited our picture of her. In her radical social idealism and the courage showed in living out those ideals with uncompromising energy, Harford foreshadows the French mystic Simone Weil. Her brief and intense life, from the little we know of it, appears to us as both tragic and fascinating. At times this biographical interest has tended to overshadow the poetry itself, as have nomen-omen remarks about her sexuality. This is exacerbated by a second factor, namely, the incidental nature and unevenness of Harford's verse. The weaker stuff has made her easy to dismiss, while her qualities may take time to come into view. This new edition aims

to encourage us to read her poetry on its own terms. It is a con-
fident selection of over half her surviving work, including many
previously unpublished poems.

Like Emily Dickinson, Harford published very little in her
lifetime. In part this may be due to the difficulty female writers
had finding a public voice amid the hullabaloo of bush ballads
and the *Bulletin*. But these poems have an intimacy of voice that
suggests Harford wrote for herself. While her social activism
required deeds, her poems arose in a different wing of the house.
They are characteristically short and have an incidental quality.
There is no context, and no attempt to universalize experience.
This minimalism is their charm and also their limitation, though
it's hard to see any shortcomings in the best of them, as here:

> Pat wasn't Pat last night at all.
> He was the rain, —
> The Spring, —
> Young Dionysus, white and warm, —
> Lilac and everything.

The idiosyncratic punctuation is another trait she shares with
Dickinson. Unlike her American forebear, however, she was no
recluse. Her inspiration was often love, and many of the poems
about her fellow factory workers have a distinct erotic charge:

> Maisie's been holding down her head all day,
> Her little red head. And her pointed chin
> Rests on her neck that slips so softly in
> The square-cut low-necked darling dress she made
> In such a way, since it's high-waisted too,
> It lets you guess how fair young breasts begin
> Under her gentle pleasant folds of blue.

There is none of the swagger of Henry Lawson, or earnestness of Mary Gilmore in Harford. At times she is closer to Blake: 'My mission in the world / Is to prolong / Rapture, by turning it / Into a song', she writes.

In her isolation from the literary currents of her day she is often coupled with John Shaw Neilson. Neilson, though twenty years her senior, would outlive Harford by another fifteen. Both are sometimes called naïve. I don't like this term. Naïve may imply an endearing naturalness, but it also condescends. Harford's best poetry goes beyond dichotomies of innocence and sophistication to be both spontaneous and artful. In order to cultivate a childlike rapture about the world, poets often keep their poetic being at one remove from the society around them.

Harford has been cited as one of our first writers to break free from the Victorian era and present the modern world in plain speech. 'Into old rhymes / New words come tripping slowly', she wrote. But come they did, and they were tied up with an urban reality, as in this poem, with its characteristic final docked line:

Sometimes the skirts I push through my machine
Spread circlewise, strong-petalled lobe on lobe,
And look for the rapt moment of a dream
Like Buddha's robe.

Often she captures the atmosphere of a vanished Melbourne: its trams and factories, its kitchen maids and absent soldiers; but also its pepper trees and eucalyptus flowers. However, she is equally able to leave the city behind and hover in a spiritual realm. Here are the first three quatrains of one of her last pieces:

I am no mystic. All the ways of God
Are dark to me.

I know not if he lived or if he died
In agony.

My every act has reference to man.
Some human need
Or this one, or of that, or of myself
Inspires the deed.

But when I hear the Angelus, I say
A Latin prayer
Hoping the dim incanted words may shine
Some way, somewhere.

A mystical visionary may not be part of our collective picture of Harford, who had renounced the Catholic faith of her upbringing, but religious elements surface often in her work, reminding us just how broad the range of this short-lived poet really was.

## Works Cited

Lesbia Harford, *Collected Poems*, ed. Oliver Dennis, UWAP 2014.

# The Green Man of the Desert: On John Wolseley

In his poem 'Australia', A.D. Hope famously wrote, 'She is the last of the lands, the emptiest'. This was 1939, but Hope's description of the centre of the continent as 'that waste' encapsulated a disconnect between the human realm and the natural environment that stretched back to the earlier European settlers, and accompanied us for most of the twentieth century. True, Hope finished by declaring an intention to turn his back on civilization and dwell like a prophet in the desert, but only once the outback had been conceived as Modernism's ideal inner landscape, a void.

At the beginning of *Heartlands and Headwaters*, the catalogue which accompanies the exhibition of recent work by John Wolseley at the National Gallery of Victoria, there is a map of Australia with a diagram superimposed to locate the eighteen remote sites that led to the major pieces on display. They stretch from Tasmania through the centre of the continent and up to encompass the flood plains of the Northern Territory. The lines connecting these sites form what Wolseley describes as 'a great tree, river, or human body'. In a way unusual for Western art in Australia the continent is envisaged as a tree of life, and hence as a vital ecosystem. 'No artist in Australia's history had ever attempted something so vast and holistic', writes Sahsa Grishin in his thorough and measured monograph *Landmarks III*, released in an extended edition to coincide with the exhibition. 'While earlier artists, including Nolan and Drysdale, when attempting to capture the heart of the Australian continent showed the arid, dry interior or the red centre, Wolseley shows an image of Australia with the life-giving waters pumping through its veins'. As the word heartland suggests, the landscapes Wolseley brings to life pulsate. In many of them, it is the centre which is most colourful and alive with the rhythms of nature.

If the tree of life is one image Wolseley sees running through the exhibition and through the continent, then the human figure standing like Da Vinci's Vitruvian Man is another. Wolseley however, prefers to imagine Pan or the Green Man. At a time when much of human existence has been separated from the natural world, such figures serve to remind us that we are 'just one part of the earth, and have deep physical and emotional connections with its fabric'. Wolseley writes:

> I see my job as a landscape artist at this critical time as being an attempt to mend some of those broken connections, as a process of healing and re-enchanting. Actually I think that some of the great landscape painters of the world did do this — they gave us a sense of oneness of earth and man.

The artist can no longer observe Nature with 'the objectivity of a cool modernist'. Landscape painting is not about possession or an escape into nature, but, as Grishin writes, it is a carrier of ideology, 'a plea for survival and the urgent need to see the earth as a sustainable system'. In a letter to the then Prime Minister Paul Keating written in 1995, Wolseley had described how he felt 'more like a war artist than a landscape artist', because he was painting in sites 'of great beauty and secrecy', 'heart areas in landscape' that were being decimated by logging. Ecological art? Yes, but one that combines political and ethical concerns with a scientific gaze, as well as being an intuitive and emotional cry for the earth. Wolseley believes a landscape should show the unity of what he terms 'livingness' — 'the energy fields made up of flocks of birds, rustling fields of reeds, flow of clouds blowing in the wind, that's what landscape is — not a collection of nouns . . . but a collection of verbs . . .'.

One of the techniques by which Wolseley has attempted to bring the modernist artist closer to the Green Man and overcome that disconnect between culture and nature, is to invite Nature to collaborate in the artistic process. His techniques include leaving sheets of paper out in the bush to be blown about and marked by the elements, rubbing paper against charcoal branches, or burying them until they show the filigree of root systems. It is through the layering or collision of such incidental markings or 'different systems' that 'I am able to make my own model of a particular landscape'. That juxtaposition of multiple visual fields can be very aesthetically pleasing. However when Wolseley asks, 'how much does the artist impose ideas on the landscape and how much is the artist a vehicle through which nature reveals herself?', it could be argued he is setting up a false dichotomy. Human nature is itself a manifestation of Nature, and as our greatest evolutionary attribute, language, demonstrates, it is in our nature to tend towards abstraction and the imposition of order. Of course if words become too abstract they lose vitality. Enter the poet, who keeps language alive and in tune with nature, not by writing frog choruses or imitations of bird song, but by naming reality carefully and lovingly, by recognising with humility our place in the world.

Wolseley's collaborations with nature seem akin in spirit to a time when artists would prepare their own pigments, or when the poet wrote with a quill. That is to say, in the artistic process there is a direct contact with the natural world and a curiosity regarding the world. It used to be said by proponents of metrical poetry in English that iambic rhythms mimicked the beating of the heart. Whether this is true or not, it expressed an admirable desire to keep the language close to reality.

These points are important to clarify because, while anthropocentrism is a real limit of our culture, particularly now when we risk destroying the planet, the uniqueness of the human perspective is our greatest strength. I disagree with Grishin's advocacy of anti-humanism in one of the two new chapters in *Landmarks III*, '*Umwelt* and the anti-humanist conception of the world'. The *umwelt* is the idea that every species inhabits its own subjective environment, each as valid as our own. It seems to me that this could be an argument in favour of our present consumer society — we are hard-wired to be 'collectively selfish', to adopt an expression from the Pope's recent encyclical on climate change. But the importance of those currents of thought loosely brought together under the term humanism, and the reason we must continue to uphold humanism's values, is that they celebrate what in the human species allows individuals to strive to a greater vision, and perceive the world from those multiple perspectives that Wolseley demonstrates admirably in his art. Renaissance Humanism, for example, should not be boiled down to the maxim 'man is the measure of all things'. It was equally Pico della Mirandola's restless positioning of man in the chain of being, just as it was Dante's similes linking human souls in an afterlife to fireflies and storks, and transforming them into trees, and just as it was a celebration of reason and imagination that reconnected the Renaissance to the past and allowed society to think forward into the future. These humanistic values gave rise to the scientific revolution. They have allowed Wolseley to envisage that tree of life superimposed on the map of our continent at the beginning of this exhibition.

Some of the most interesting aspects of Cathy Leahy's fine catalogue to accompany the National Gallery of Victoria *Heartlands and Headwaters* exhibition, are the descriptions by Wolseley that accompany each of the major works. Many describe the moment of conception when the land seemed to reveal something of its secrets, 'an instant of seeing into the life of things'. They are also eloquent in charting his artistic vision, as when he writes, 'I have tried to show how landscape for me is made up of energy fields rendered as passages of particular plant forms, in which the individual plants move or dance with different rhythms'.

If the paintings capture different rhythms, they also embody different times. Wolseley talks of three distinct time perspectives at work in his vision, 'the deep time of geology, shallow time since European arrival, and now time'. Of 'From the edge of the great flood plains of Garrangari and Garrangali, NT', he writes:

> for me the great miracle of that morning . . . rested in that moment in time — being there, seeing the living land and sensing the 'deep time' so intimately linked in partnership and correspondence with the life, art and religion of the people who have lived in it for so long.

It's not always a celebration, however. For another piece the artist travelled with indigenous elder Brownie Doolan, one of the last speakers of Lower Arrernte, to his ancestral lands deep in the Simpson desert. At a certain point, 'a grasshopper landed on my knee. Brownie said its name — 'ngarr ngarr' — in a soft voice, and I thought that is probably, after thousands of years, the last time this word will hang in the desert air'.

Wolseley is also careful in these descriptions to set out the processes and techniques behind the work. In the painting 'Mallee gilgai' for example art as mimesis is given fresh legs in the following:

> I laid out huge sheets of paper on the banks of sandhills and started in a rather wild and physical way by pouring, brushing and sploshing quantities of watercolour that I had previously mixed up in large bowls. All those watery landscape elements around me were then recreated on the paper. Pools in depressions on the paper overflowed in slow, winding rivulets and became an analogue of what hydrologists call 'chain of pond systems'.

In the heat of the sun 'the pigments . . . thickened and sometimes caked and cracked — the way mud does in a drying water pool'. He found 'that more than ever before this process of making a watercolour seemed to be analogous to the action and process by which water itself moves and forms the landscape'. Wolseley has written that he aims to find ways to receive from and listen to Nature, and also that his work 'has often been a meditation on alternative ways of imagining land — the matrix in which we live'. In these two publications that important vision has been given new life.

## Works Cited

*John Wolseley Heartlands and Headwaters* by Cathy Leahy, with contributions by Helen McDonald and John Wolseley, National Gallery of Victoria, 2015.

*John Wolseley Landmarks III* by Sasha Grishin, Thames and Hudson, 2015.

# The Poet of History:
## On Czesław Miłosz

.......................................................

'I have no hesitation whatsoever in stating that Czesław Miłosz is
one of the greatest poets of our time, perhaps the greatest', wrote
Joseph Brodsky in 1978. Yet two years later when the sixty-nine-
year-old Miłosz (1911–2004) was awarded the Nobel prize for
literature, most people were hearing his name for the first time.
For three decades prior to 1980 he had been living in exile, first
in France, then the United States. His books were banned in
Poland, and his reputation as a poet survived on a small read-
ership of the émigré Polish community and thanks to the help
of some hard-working English translators. He was known if
at all as a political scientist due to *The Captive Mind*, his bril-
liant portrayal of the psychological pressure to conform faced
by intellectuals under totalitarian communism. So who was this
Lithuanian-born poet who wrote in Polish, and what makes him
one of the most important writers of the twentieth century?

Until his forties Miłosz lived in what he referred to ironically
as that 'other Europe'. Eastern Europe, and Poland particularly,
caught between Russia and the Nazis, and then caged behind

the Iron Curtain, were to witness some of the worst upheavals of the twentieth century. Here people were to feel the brunt of that fickle and uncontrollable force Miłosz personified as History. Like its medieval counterpart, Fortune, History would overturn at will entire communities and even nations.

He was born in Szetejnie, Lithuania. His family 'thought of themselves as Polish, but they aligned themselves with the Grand Duchy of Lithuania'. This already introduces a complexity of identity, a multicultural, multilingual experience that was at odds with the concept of the nation state that would be imposed on so many parts of Europe like a straight-jacket. Like Yugoslavia at the end of last century, the area of Miłosz's youth suffered terribly. Vilnius, that city of magnificent baroque churches, that was also know as the Jerusalem of the North for its large and vibrant Jewish population, was where Miłosz attended school and university. It would change hands thirteen times over the course of the twentieth century.

When the Nobel did come, it coincided with the beginning of a change of fortune for Poland. 1980 was two years after the election of another Pole, Pope John Paul II, to the Vatican. It was also the year the anti-communist social movement Solidarity was born at the Gdańsk Shipyards. Suddenly Poland was making people in the West take notice of the experiences of those 'second-class Europeans'. Thanks to translation, Western writers became aware of a whole community of other European intellectuals whose moral engagement with the historical forces of their century offered a fresh antidote to the West's own navel-gazing — writers like Herbert, Szymborska, Popa and Haclav. By the time of his death, Fortune's wheel had turned for Miłosz. Poland, which had once banned his books, now considered him one of its greatest heroes.

Andrzej Franaszek's biography, first issued in Poland in 2011, has now been translated and edited by Aleksandra and Michael Parker and published by Harvard. It is a good guide to Miłosz, his writings, and his complex encounters with History. In its English embodiment, it is a pleasure to read.

'To express the existential situation of modern man one must live in exile of some sort' Miłosz wrote. That instability and longing for the Lithuania of his youth would be a constant theme of his writing. In two prose works, *The Issa Valley* and *Native Realm*, he would bring that world to life in ecstatic celebration. He was well aware that it was an earthly paradise to which there could be no return.

In the 1930s he was living in Warsaw. Under the Nazi occupation people were in constant danger of simply disappearing. It was here in the spring of 1943 that the Jewish Ghetto uprising was repressed, described by Miłosz in a piece previously unpublished in English:

> on a beautiful quiet night, a country night in the outskirts of Warsaw, standing on the balcony, we could hear screaming from the ghetto . . . This screaming gave us goose pimples. They were the screams of thousands of people being murdered. It travelled through the silent spaces of the city from among a red glow of fires, under indifferent stars, into the benevolent silence of gardens in which plants laboriously emitted oxygen, the air was fragrant, and a man felt that it was good to be alive. There was something particularly cruel in this peace of the night, whose beauty and human crime struck the heart simultaneously. We did not look each other in the eye.

The surreal contrast between human suffering and our instinct for joy is typical of Miłosz's poetry. What is the role of poetry amidst such suffering? he asks in a poem from 1945 entitled 'Dedication':

> What is poetry which does not save
> Nations or people?
> A connivance with official lies,
> A song of drunkards whose throats will be cut in a moment,
> Readings for sophomore girls.

And yet Miłosz was simultaneously drawn to praise the wonder of the world, the desire to divine the spiritual in the things of sense. That struggle between the individual life of the poet and his role as witness to History can never go away:

> It's madness to live without joy
> And to repeat to the dead
> Whose part was to be gladness
> Of action in thought and in the flesh, singing, feasts,
> Only the two salvaged words:
> Truth and justice.

At the end of the Second World War Miłosz made a choice which was to earn him many enemies in Polish émigré communities. He collaborated with the new communist government in Poland, obtaining a coveted diplomatic role as cultural attaché. Despite the clear signs that the Polish People's Republic was little more than a Soviet puppet, Miłosz continued in this role until 1950. He then sought exile in France.

Franaszek does an excellent job of describing this complex period in Poland's history, and the depth of existential angst Miłosz faced in making his decision. For the poet, exile is never easy — for what is a poet without his language? The support of Jerzy Giedroyc, editor of the Polish émigré literary and political magazine *Kultura* based in Paris, seems to have been vital. For the first three years Miłosz's wife and two young children were stuck in the United States. He hoped to join them, but was denied a visa due to his communist allegiances. It was not until 1960 that he returned to the United States, when the Department of Slavic Languages at Berkley offered him a lectureship. He would remain in California for most of this later part of his life.

The Nobel committee statement emphasised the ethical elements of Miłosz's work, and the life-time resistance to forces of evil and havoc. For the first half of his life up until his exile in 1951 those forces were decidedly political. As Michael Parker writes in a useful introduction, Miłosz 'counters the communist orthodoxy that human beings are solely products of blind historical forces and ideological conditioning, by re-asserting their status as beings possessed of a 'soul''.

Once he reached the United States, that counter broadened to include a resistance to artistic forces, particularly those of nihilism and relativism. Asked in a *Paris Review* interview why he wrote, Miłosz stated, 'I follow my need for rhythm and order, and my struggle against chaos and nothingness to translate as many aspects as possible of reality into form'. Elsewhere, he wrote, 'the ideal occupation for a poet is the contemplation of the word "is"'. His work has a metaphysical element that is refreshing and a challenge to the empirical pessimism of our age. He sought a revelation of reality, where the concrete and the spiritual sit alongside each other: 'Artists crave being, a communion with the divine promise inside creation'. Are such visions romantic escapism? His poetry is full of self-deprecating irony, but it never strays into the sarcasm and bleakness of Philip Larkin. Take, for example, his poem 'Incantation'. Despite the title, the fervour and sense of hope are palpable:

Human reason is beautiful and invincible.
No bars, no barbed wire, no pulping of books,
No sentence of banishment can prevail against it.
It establishes the universal ideas in language,
And guides our hand so we write Truth and Justice
With capital letters, lie and oppression with small.
. . .
Beautiful and very young are Philo-Sophia
And poetry, her ally in the service of the good.
As late as yesterday Nature celebrated their birth,
The news was brought to the mountains by a unicorn and an
    echo.
Their friendship will be glorious, their time has no limit.
Their enemies have delivered themselves to destruction.

Asking himself why twentieth-century poetry had such a gloomy and apocalyptical tone in his Charles Eliot Norton lectures, *The Witness of Poetry*, Miłosz identified 'the progressing subjectivization that becomes manifest when we are imprisoned in the melancholy of our individual transience'. This has led to a 'separation of the poet from the great human family'. Ironically, it was History, not as modern-day Fortune, but as engagement with our cultural patrimony, that Miłosz came to see as vital for reconnecting with that human family. One of his favourite quotes was from Japanese poet Issa: 'We walk on the roof of Hell, gazing at flowers'. This double perception of life is the strength of Miłosz's work.

## Works Cited

Andrzej Franaszek, *Miłosz: A Biography*, ed. and trans. Aleksandra and Michael Parker, Harvard University Press, 2017.

# Oracles and the Intellect: James McAuley in the Centenary of his Birth

·················································································

'It was a pretty idle afternoon in Victoria Barracks', McAuley would later say. 'I suppose we must have started about lunchtime.' What followed is well known. In October 1943 two young poets, James McAuley and Harold Stewart created the fictitious poet Ern Malley, whose slim manuscript of surreal poems, *The Darkening Ecliptic*, they sent to Max Harris and his magazine *Angry Penguins*. The idea was to ridicule this new movement of 'garish images without coherent meaning and structure'. McAuley famously described how:

> we produced the whole of Ern Malley's tragic life-work in one afternoon, with the aid of a chance collection of books . . . opened at random, choosing a word or a phrase haphazardly. We made lists of these and wove them into nonsensical sentences. We misquoted and made false allusion.

The hoax succeeded. Max Harris dedicated a special issue, with a cover image by Sidney Nolan, to this sensational new talent.

When the ruse was uncovered, Harris faced ridicule and was even tried in the courts for obscenity, a twist more absurd than the poems themselves. And yet Malley would not be laid to rest.

McAuley and Stewart had asserted that 'the writings of Ern Malley are utterly devoid of literary merit as poetry'. Malley seemed determined to prove his creators wrong. He took on a life of his own, overshadowing the poetic careers of both his inventors. At the conclusion of the opening and best poem in *The Darkening Ecliptic*, 'Dürer: Innsbruck, 1495' Malley had described himself as 'the black swan of trespass on alien waters'. But the movement McAuley and Stewart had ridiculed would turn out to be one of the dominant strands of modernism, and Malley would be perfectly at home in the twentieth century.

It was James McAuley who was the black swan of his times. This year marks the centenary of his birth in 1917. He would have been disappointed that a commemorative essay began with the hoax. He was in his mid twenties at the time. He had not yet published a book, and his best poetry was still to be written. It was a youthful joke, before the serious work began. But where else could we begin? McAuley's ensuing career can be read as a struggle to justify that claim that Malley was 'utterly devoid of literary merit'. As modernism in its various manifestations became the dominant cultural voice, Malley became the epitome of everything McAuley would react against. McAuley announced his alternative vision for the age, sometimes as a combative reactionary, sometimes as a prophet calling from the wilderness. His poem 'In the Twentieth Century' begins:

Christ, you walked on the sea,
But cannot walk in a poem,
Not in our century.

There's something deeply wrong
Either with us or with you.

Now as we climb out of the twentieth century by our own boot-straps, does McAuley's alternative vision have anything to offer?

Because Malley is at the crux of it all, let me delve a little deeper. Malley's poem 'Sybilline' begins:

That rabbit's foot I carried in my left pocket
Has worn a haemorrhage in the lining
The bunch of keys I carry with it
Jingles like fate in my omphagic ear
And when I stepped clear of the solid basalt
The introverted obelisk of night
I seized upon this Traumdeutung as a sword
To hew a passage to my love.

In these lines there are echoes of the symbolist poet Christopher Brennan, on whom McAuley had written his MA a few years earlier. The voice is also similar to a poem like 'The Blue Horses' in McAuley's first volume of poetry *Under Aldebaran* published a few years later in 1946:

What loud wave-motioned hooves awaken
Our dream-fast members from the cramp of sleep?
The tribal images are shaken
And crash upon their guardians. The skies
Are shivered like a pane of glass.

What both these passages have is a surety of voice, a voice that commands authority, invites us to trust it, even where we may not understand everything it is saying. But early on in his career

McAuley came to consider that authority bogus. It was the voice of the sophist.

Sophism was the reason for Plato's famous dislike of poetry. Plato considered poets to be peddlers of rhetoric who had freed language of responsibility to reason and truth. Was Plato too pedantic? He was certainly harsh to lump all poets in such a category, and unjust in his reluctance to accept that truth and reason might have plains of expression beyond that of logic. Poetry, the real stuff, does aim at truth, but recognises that we can't pin it down for long, just as words cannot be riveted into place like eternal forms. There is in Auden's justification for cutting his poem 'September 1, 1939' something Platonic: it doesn't matter how pretty it sounds, if it is untrue it's a bad poem.

In a statement made about Ern Malley in 1960 McAuley recalled:

at that time there was a pretty big surge, in poetry and in the arts generally, of what I would call a wave of surrender to irrational forces. Now, there are lots of ways of describing this. One way I think would be to say that it was a quarrel over the nature of inspiration. I think there are in fact two sorts of process that lead to productions which purport to be artistic, and I would call one pseudo-inspiration and the other one genuine inspiration. And I think pseudo-inspiration is precisely the excitement of this surrender to irrational forces. It's a devaluation of the capacities of consciousness in artistic production and an over-valuation, and over-reliance, on what can come up from the depths. It's a matter of consulting the oracle in the unconscious cave. . . . Genuine inspiration I take to be an action of the whole man. . . . It is not a matter of excluding the energies and the imagery thrown up by the unconscious, but it is a matter of using all one's resources, including the sovereign power of the shaping intellect.

Faith in the sovereign power of intellect places McAuley as a quester for poetic truth. In his 1959 collection of essays *The End of Modernity* McAuley associated this pseudo-inspiration with the concept of art for art's sake, where rhetoric, which is the art of verbal communication, has broken free of its intellectual responsibilities and is degraded 'into sophistic, the art of verbal gratification and display'.

The twentieth century lost faith in the intellect for a number of reasons, and not all artists were willing to share McAuley's claim that despite its limitations, reason was a god-given gift to be nourished rather than ridiculed. As children of that century it is sobering to be reminded of the limitations of our inheritance, something *The End of Modernity* foretold.

What is that inheritance? For McAuley poetry had become disconnected from its social role. The isolation of aesthetic motives in art for art's sake, far from being the natural and original condition of art:

> is rather to be considered a perversion and decadence, and a sure sign of the approaching exhaustion of cultural vitality. A veritable cult of originality arises precisely at the point where art, having been fully 'emancipated' becomes unable to originate any style of its own, but is driven to a restless creation of novelties by the elaboration of syncretisation and parody.

For McAuley it's not the intellect alone that will fix poetry's social role. There's the heart too. 'In the old symbolism the heart was the principal organ, the seat of life, soul, intellect, memory, will. It is as it were the gathering together of the powers of the mind into that unity which we speak of as "I"'. Thus, in 'An Art of Poetry' he writes:

Scorn then to darken and contract
The landscape of the heart
By individual, arbitrary
And self-expressive art.

Let your speech be ordered wholly
By an intellectual love;
Elucidate the carnal maze
With clear light from above.

These days it requires mental effort to acknowledge the distinction such lines make between the landscape of the heart on the one hand, and all that is individual, and self-expressive. McAuley's landscape requires one to look outwards from the self, towards what is common rather than what is idiosyncratic. Similarly, in 'Credo' he writes:

The meaning not ours, but found
In the mind deeply submissive
To the grammar of existence,
The syntax of the real

Why deeply? Does he mean down to the bedrock of belief? Or is he talking about that marriage of heart and intellect, the poetic truth, to set against Plato's rationality? If so then this quatrain belies the stereotype of McAuley as a throwback to the English eighteenth century.

What role might poetry have then? 'Poetry lives closer to the metaphysical centre; its symbolisms are more nearly primal and universal'. *The End of Modernity* is a lament for a vanishing metaphysical dimension in literature. It is as if the landscape of the heart were able to transport the intellect into a realm of archetypes:

it is poetry with its musical power and its greater access to the myths and symbols associated with man's deepest longings, that can most richly assert against the modern world the true values of the spirit. Poetry continually tends to revive in man the sense of what makes him authentic.

The importance of this metaphysical dimension becomes clear when McAuley takes aim at its opposite, those artists who 'fall into a state of nescience about their own intellectual assumptions and allegiances'. This leads to envisaging the writing of poetry as a sort of play of an unattached sensibility, where the materials of poetry are like a 'confetti of sense-impressions whirled about by little gusts of feeling'.

The references to myths and symbols remind us that McAuley kept in touch with his early interest in symbolism. Like Yeats, McAuley saw poetry as an antidote to the naturalism, scientism and materialism of modernity. Unlike Yeats, he is sceptical of the Imagination. Blake could write 'the world of imagination is the world of Eternity. It is the Divine bosom into which we shall all go after the death of the vegetated body. The world of imagination is infinite and eternal.' Yeats agreed, and put his finger on the heart of the issue at the end of his essay 'Symbolism in Painting':

> one must determine what value to give to the imagination. Is it an alternative to the lost metaphysical certainties of religion, and a way of keeping in touch with an archetypal realm? Does imagination tap into the 'eternal realities'? Or is it merely a momentary dream, an escape into idiosyncratic vision and madness?

Yeats knew his mind on this subject. McAuley was more wary. Horatio, after all, had used imagination as a synonym for madness in this description of Hamlet, 'he waxes desperate with imagination'. Similarly, Theseus says in *A Midsummer Night's Dream*:

> The poet's eye, in a fine frenzy rolling
> doth glance from heaven to earth, from earth to heaven
> and as imagination bodies forth
> the forms of things unknown, the poet's pen
> turns them to shapes and give to aery nothing
> a local habitation and a name.

The danger of imagination is its independence from reality, for without reality we have no common ground. Yet imagination is necessary, for it has the potential to enrich and transform cool reason's thin reality. When Hippolyta replies to Theseus, she says the trick is to make the poet's fantasies through art, 'grow to something of great constancy'. Would McAuley have agreed? The factor which he believed distinguished his ideas from Blake, is imagination's ultimate 'submission to reality'. 'It is not an individual idiosyncratic enterprise. It finds truths rather than contrives them'. On the basis of this perceived distinction, McAuley dismisses Yeats as a peddler of 'spiritual-cultural make-believe'.

*

McAuley was born in the Sydney suburb of Lakemba in 1917. He was a scholarship boy at Sydney University, where he wrote his masters thesis, 'Symbolism: An Essay in Poetics', in 1940. In 1943 he was commissioned as lieutenant into the Australian army, serving in Melbourne (the Victoria Barracks that gave rise to Malley), and Canberra. After the war he continued in the army where he worked in New Guinea. In 1952 he converted to Roman Catholicism, the faith his father had abandoned. He went on to be one of the most fiery and outspoken Catholic intellectuals of his day. In 1956 he founded together with Richard Krygier the literary and cultural magazine *Quadrant*, where he was chief editor until 1963. In 1961 he became professor of English at the University of Tasmania. He remained in Hobart until his death from cancer in 1976, aged 59.

McAuley's ideas of the social role of poetry were closely connected to the way the artist relates to the tradition. It is through an engagement with the tradition that one learns to get beyond a cult of individualism and emotional idiosyncrasy, as Eliot had announced in 'Tradition and the Individual Talent'. But modernism and its offshoots were to have troubled relations with those traditions. It's not hard to imagine McAuley taking aim at works like *The Cantos* in this quote:

> For the traditional artist originality has nothing to do with novelty or individual idiosyncrasy; it means making the tradition one's own, by re-creating it at each moment in one's own spirit. This does not mean an absence of borrowing of motifs, though it is opposed to the curio-work, the kleptomania, and the necrophilia of arts that live on sensations.

I'm left wondering how one can distinguish between cherry-picking from the past, and an abiding recreation of traditions in one's own spirit. McAuley doesn't address this question as directly as I would have liked. What he does enunciate very clearly throughout *The End of Modernity* is a perceived danger when the real world is abolished in favour of a world of poetry's own making, when the poet transforms rhetoric to sophistry, or when he turns

his back on the past, in short when the twentieth century com-
mits what he calls 'The Magian Heresy'

*

In turning to McAuley's own poetry for alternatives to what he
had so passionately denounced in *The End of Modernity*, I find
myself disappointed. Not that the poetry is bad. His best work
is excellent and deserves a central place in the history of our
mid twentieth-century literature. But it is excellent in ways that
are unexpected from the author of those fiery essays, and it was
not until later in his career that he found that voice. Up until
the mid-sixties McAuley's preferred mode in poetry and prose
was the polemic, what Les Murray calls his 'scornful Sydney
University debating style'. In the 'Prologue' to the first issue of
*Quadrant* he wrote with characteristic divisiveness, 'We shall try
to be liberal and progressive, without falling into the delusion
that to be liberal and progressive means to rehearse with childish
obstinacy the rituals of a sentimental and neurotic leftism.' The
poetry written up to and during the same period and collected
in *Under Alderbaran* (1946) and *A Vision of Ceremony* (1956)
tends to a similar tone, most famously in the heroic couplets of
'A Letter to John Dryden':

> But these on whom my anguish lingers most,
> The disinherited and anxious host
> Of half-way-decent simple stunted souls,
> What hidden principle is it controls
> Their creedless thoughts? What flag hangs on their poles?
> It may be no one principle indeed,
> But unexamined shreds of every creed;
> And certainly their minds contain a hash
> Of random notions in a tasteless mash

The dismissive and generalising tone here is more distasteful than what he takes aim at. There is a proselytising streak in McAuley that worked against him. 'Take salt upon the tongue. / And do not feed the heart / With sorrow, darkness or lies', he wrote in 'To Any Poet' — but most of the salt seemed to be issuing from his own pen.

There are signs in this period of the more personal tone which was to come later. Take for example, 'Late Winter', in McAuley's favourite form, the quatrain, and quoted whole:

The pallid cuckoo
Sent up in frail
Microtones
His tiny scale

On the cold air.
What joy I found
Mounting that tiny
Stair of sound.

'Late Winter' could be set anywhere. When McAuley turns to Australia as a subject, the portrayal is in the tradition of Hope's 'nation of trees, drab green and desolate grey'. Take 'Bush Scene', for example, which begins:

Harsh, dry, abrasive, spiky, rough,
Untidy, tattered, irregular:
Beauty is not a word you'd choose
For what's most characteristic here.

The poem goes on to claim, 'by no stretch is it a *locus amoenus*'. Despite the disparaging tone, I take heart reading this now. It reminds me how far our poetry has come in the last fifty years.

We have now learnt to tune our sensibilities to our landscapes. The generic title, 'Bush Scene', would never do today. Our poets have found ways to celebrate the continent's natural environments. If it is hard to consider those landscapes as *loci amoeni*, then the fault lies not in the land itself so much as our uneasy relationship with it; and where they are celebrated as such, they are not subservient to the classical Western trope, but grow out of it to become something unique. It is also a reminder of just how important Judith Wright was in these decades.

From the mid-fifties until its publication in 1964, McAuley channelled much of his poetic energies into *Captain Quiros*. Perhaps the best way to describe *Quiros* is as a mini-epic. It adopts the tropes and themes of the epic poem, as well as a formal tone, and yet it is only seventy pages long. The poem is an account in rhyme royal (rhyming either ABABCCB, or ABABCCA) of the two unsuccessful voyages by Portuguese navigator Pedro Fernandes de Queirós (1565–1614) across the Pacific Ocean in search of Terra Australis. McAuley emphasises Quiros' fervent Catholicism so that the voyage becomes a search 'to win for Christ the Southern Continent'. It was not well-received at the time, and has subsequently struggled to gain attention. McAuley, or at least his fictional narrator, Belmonte, does not have a knack for creating memorable characters. Despite the interest of events themselves, the poem struggles with pacing and is not good at evoking scenes.

It would be wrong however to ignore *Quiros*, for its hero in his crusading role is McAuley himself:

Our voyage was to be a solemn rite,
A passing through the waters to rebirth
In a new world, created in despite
Of the demonic powers that rule the age.

Those demonic powers recall the age denounced in *The End of Modernity*. McAuley, like Quiros, pits himself against his times. When Belmonte says 'I play a match against the age's mind: / The board is set; the living pieces move', it is impossible not to see the parallel with McAuley.

The parallel is important because at the end of the poem Quiros accepts the misguidedness of his unrealised ambitions. Returning after the second failed journey Quiros asks the dying Father Commissary, who had accompanied the ships, why God had denied them. This is what Quiros is told:

> He lapsed through weakness. Then he spoke once more:
> 'Conformed to Christ in longing, we aspire
> to re-create creation, and restore
> All things in Justice, perfect and entire:
> This is indeed our task and privilege;
> This in our voyage was our sacred pledge,
> Yet under limits we may not ignore.
>
> 'For in the midst of time God has not willed
> The End of Time. Nor ours to bring to birth
> That final Realm; nor shall our labours build
> Out of the rubble of this fallen earth
> The New Jerusalem . . .

These are wise words to set against the intellectual hubris of Quiros/McAuley. They are also a recognition of a bridge between the desires of Quiros/McAuley to 're-create creation', and those artists such as Yeats and Rilke who had been denounced in *The End of Modernity* for the Magian Heresy, that is replacing God with themselves as creators of their own worlds. Quiros was ready to see the errors of his way:

In Quiros' soul a troubled echo sounded:
'That even perfection is a snare, I see;
Yet by the gospel word I am confounded:
*Be ye perfect.* Was it fault in me
That with intense desire I sought to escape
This blind world's evil so far as to shape
Our labours to a secular liturgy?'

A little later, now on his own death-bed, Quiros comes to accept the limits of the secular age he finds himself in. He turns away from the proselytiser and associates the just with a quieter spirituality:

Now in a time of loneliness and dearth
The just shall live by faith without the aid
Of custom that bound man to heaven and earth.
Estranged within the city man has made,
Like smoke of sacrifice they shall arise,
Or vapour drawn up swiftly to the skies,
Unknown or counted as of little worth.

This is a melancholy and lonely vision of the artist. McAuley would make this same turn away from combativeness in his next volume, *Surprises of the Sun*, 1969.

*Surprises of the Sun*, contains most of McAuley's best poems, many of which are very good indeed. Vincent Buckley had written of McAuley's earlier work, and the comment is applicable to everything up to *Surprises*, that it wasn't 'earthy enough . . . there is too little flesh to afford incarnation to the word'. Les Murray describes it as 'pruned of all emotion except perhaps angry combativeness'. Suddenly, he had found a way to transform the persona of public intellectual that had dominated his poetry. He bows his humble head, and writes poems that 'make no comment', as in 'Childhood Morning — Homebush:

The half-moon is a muted lamp
Motionless behind a veil.
As the eastern sky grows pale,
I hear the slow-train's puffing stamp

Gathering speed. A bulbul sings,
Raiding persimmon and fig.
The rooster in full glossy rig
Crows triumph at the state of things.

I make no comment; I don't know;
I don't know what there is to know.
I hear that every answer's No,
But can't believe it can be so.

The voice of *vates* is replaced by that of an individual talking to a lover or a god. It has become common to see *Surprises* as a surprise, arriving out of the blue. Leonie Kramer, who edited a useful anthology of McAuley's work for UQP in 1988, is right to point out that the new direction was neither wholly new, nor a simple rejection of his intellectual rigour for confessionalism. The fine early poem 'Celebration of Love' suggests what was *in potentia*. And yet there is a new humility, an ability to confess 'I cannot understand', learnt from *Captain Quiros*.

Many of the best poems in *Surprises* return to McAuley's childhood, such as 'Because' and 'Wisteria', 'Tabletalk' and 'Soundings'. The note of contrition is strong. Who would have thought the author of 'A Letter to John Dryden' would come to write the following:

People do what they can; they were good people,
They cared for us and loved us. Once they stood
Tall in my childhood as the school, the steeple.
How can I judge without ingratitude?

Judgement is simply trying to reject
A part of what we are because it hurts.

Then there is 'Pietà', which though I've read it countless times
still gives me goose bumps:

A year ago you came
Early into the light.
You lived a day and night,
Then died; no-one to blame.

Once only, with one hand,
Your mother in farewell
Touched you. I cannot tell,
I cannot understand

A thing so dark and deep,
So physical a loss:
One touch, and that was all

She had of you to keep.
Clean wounds, but terrible,
Are those made with the Cross.

In 1975, the year before his death, McAuley published *A Map of Australian Verse*, an anthology I found very useful when starting out as a poet. In the introduction to the section dedicated to his own poems he makes repeated reference to having followed 'an inner necessity' and 'a path intuitively sensed and dimly descried', before summarising his career as 'the persistent desire to write poems that are lucid and mysterious, gracefully simple but full of secrets, faithful to the little one knows and the much one has to feel'. No mention of the intellect here. Is it too far fetched to see in this return to mystery a reconnection with Malley? In 'Dürer: Innsbruck, 1495' after all he had written:

> I had read in books that art is not easy
> But no one warned that the mind repeats
> In its ignorance the vision of others. I am still
> The black swan of trespass on alien waters.

Perhaps we should leave the final words to McAuley's other alter ego, Quiros:

> For me the watch is past, the night is done;
> However men report when I am gone,
> The travail of my soul is satisfied.

## Works Cited

Leonie Kramer, *James McAuley, Poetry, Essays, and Personal Commentary*, University of Queensland Press, 1988.

Ern Malley, *Collected Poems*, Angus and Robertson, 1993.

James McAuley, *The End of Modernity*, Angus and Robertson, 1959.

James McAuley, *A Map of Australian Verse: The Twentieth Century*, Oxford University Press, 1975.

James McAuley, *The Grammar of the Real*, Oxford University Press, 1975.

James McAuley, *Collected Poems*, Angus and Robertson, 1994.

Les Murray, *Fivefathers*, Carcanet, 1994.

# Rosemary Dobson and the Continuance of Poetry

Dante opens his Latin treaty *De Monarchia* with the image of a tree that grows beside a river bank:

> *Omnium hominum quos ad amorem veritatis natura superior impressit hoc maxime interesse videtur: ut, quemadmodum de labore antiquorum ditati sunt, ita et ipsi posteri prolaborent, quatenus ab eis posteritas habeat quo ditetur. Longe nanque ab offitio se esse non dubitet qui, publicis documentis imbutus, ad rem publicam aliquid afferre non curat; non enim est lignum, quod secus decursus aquarum fructificat in tempore suo, sed potius perniciosa vorago semper ingurgitans et nunquam ingurgitata refundens.*

All men to whom their superior nature has given a desire to love truth should be concerned above all with this thought: that just as they have been enriched by the labours of past generations, so too they have a duty to labour for posterity in order that future generations may be enriched by their work. For without doubt he who was nurtured on past teachings concerning the common good, but does not care to contribute to society, is far from being that tree that grows by the river and brings forth its

161

fruit in the right season. Rather he is a destructive whirlpool who devours without giving anything in return.

I'm fond of that image of the flourishing tree. It is so characteristic of Dante's long vision, yoking classical and Christian traditions while stretching its sight into the future by reminding us of our responsibility to continue to transmit the flood of knowledge. The image is taken from the first simile to appear in the *Psalms* — the man who follows God is like a tree planted beside a river which yields its fruits in season and whose leaf never withers. In Milton's translation the apparent disorder of the *Old Testament* original (the parallelism that structures such ancient Hebrew song was not observed until the eighteenth century) has been ordered into heroic couplets:

He shall be as a tree which planted grows
By watery streams, and in his season knows
To yield his fruit, and his leaf shall not fall,
And what he takes in hand shall prosper all.

In the quote from *De monarchia* the river no longer stands for divine law (though Dante may have expected readers to have that in the back of their minds), but rather the artistic legacy of our forebears, the cumulative knowledge of the past as it comes down to us in cultural traditions and works of literature. In this way he links the image of personal growth to the classical topos of the thirst for knowledge.

Dante is evoking his own sense of obligation to continue to transmit knowledge for future generations. He makes this even clearer in the next image by recalling the parable of the talents — our heritage is a treasure to be invested rather than hidden away. The opening is a conceit to justify the writing of *De Monarchia*, but what interests me more is the way it balances the past with the future. It reminds us that poetry doesn't arise out of nothing. As I quoted in a previous essay, Robert Gray in his poem 'To a Friend' says, 'In writing, it wasn't renown I was after; / it seemed instead an offering to one's ancestors'. Dante reminds us that poems are both offerings to our ancestors and prayers for our children.

This might all sound obvious and unremarkable. And yet it is an idea that has continued to strike me as important and in need of fresh articulation and defence, at least in my own mind. When I ask myself why this is the case, the answer I return to involves what might be called the tyranny of the present moment. In Australia we used to suffer as a result of our geographical isolation from the tyranny of distance. We were of course isolated only in so far as our bearing points were seen to lie in England and the United States rather than Asia. Might we not struggle in a similar way to hold onto the past and our links with traditions? In our contemporary poetry the dominant voice seems to focus on a flow of sense data — what Rosemary Dobson, to whom I will return later in this essay, calls *I* poetry. *I* poetry 'concentrates on the poet's own emotions and responses . . . and assumes poetry can be created out of a void'. What she is talking about are poems that chart the reflections and changing light on the surface of Dante's river, without delving into its waters or feeling the tug of its current on our toes.

When I try to enunciate these ideas the artwork 'Cultural Rubble' comes to mind. It is a sculpture by Christine O'Loughlin, incorporated into the facade of the Ian Potter Museum of Art at the University of Melbourne. The work is made up of four panels, each representing fragmentary signs from categories of classical art — sculpture, pottery, and architecture. The panels were conceived as a site-specific work to fill four window spaces of an art centre. They were installed in 1993, and moved to their present location when the Ian Potter Museum was built in 1998. In her pitch the artist wrote: 'I propose to block those four windows . . . from the exterior with plaster-like fragments of sculpture and architecture from the European classical past. I would like to indicate . . . that the history of Australian contemporary art is based on these cultural fragments from Europe'. The use of fragments will 'reinforce the feeling of distance from the original culture'. Furthermore, the fragments 'will seem to burst from the windows to indicate that the rooms behind are used for contemporary cultural activities'. An informative essay provided by the museum claims 'Cultural Rubble' invites us 'to discard the European traditions upon which much of our cultural history is based to make way for distinctly Australian art'.

This defenestration enacts a dynamic which has played a prominent role in twentieth-century literature: the rejection of the past in favour of the new. In blocking the window, the past occludes what should really be before our eyes. It is significant that O'Loughlin speaks of fragments and rubble, and distance from the classical artworks. The fragment is deracinated and isolated from a living cultural context. It becomes a commodity in cultural exchange, another sign to be picked up and interpreted at will. 'Cultural Rubble' is often cited as one of the first post-modern public sculptures in Melbourne. The fragment is decontextualized, and reincorporated through irony and parody in the multi-vocal surface play of the new artwork. I would argue that 'Cultural Rubble' exemplifies a widespread attitude to the European cultural heritage by Australian artists and writers of its time, that is, as something to throw off or to plunder.

I have come to see my own work in opposition to these atti-
tudes. And I have tried to ask, how can we engage with the past
and our varied cultural traditions in more meaningful ways?

I am aware that I have been making reference to the past and
our literary traditions as a value in themselves, without examining what I mean by this nebulous term. The danger of evoking
it as some abstract force for good is that our gesture at conserva-
tion appears rather as a cry for conservatism and to be motivated
by a fear of change. It is Wordsworth who sums up this common
heritage I have been discussing in the *Preface* to *Lyrical Ballads*
when he describes a vast empire of human society of which the
poet must be the custodian. Importantly this empire has not
only geographical but temporal reach:

> [the poet] is the rock of defence for human nature; an upholder
> and preserver, carrying everywhere with him relationship and
> love. In spite of difference of soil and climate, of language and
> manners, of laws and customs: in spite of things silently gone
> out of mind, and things violently destroyed; the Poet binds
> together by passion and knowledge the vast empire of human
> society, as it is spread over the whole earth, and over all time.

It is significant that Wordsworth's poet must actively adopt both
passion and knowledge in order to bind together what would
otherwise be disparate. It is not the fear of change that motivates
Wordsworth here, but the fear of only looking in one direction.

In this essay I want to look briefly at Yeats, and show the
ways in which he might complement Dante's nourishing river. I
then want to discuss the poetry of Rosemary Dobson as exem-
plifying what she calls the continuance of poetry. I would use
metaphors not of rubble, but rather of bedrock and wellspring.
Or, to change the metaphoric field, I would invite us to seek

poems that are well-rooted in the humus of our literary culture. Humus reminds us that our word *culture* comes from the Latin *colere* meaning the tilling of the land, the caring for the land so that it will continue to bear fruit. In this way we get beyond the limits of the individual and idiosyncratic, the restless mania for what is new simply for the sake of novelty.

In Yeats we find the poetic vocation presented as a struggle away from the idiosyncratic and towards a communion with those deeper and more universal parts of ourselves. Unlike Wordsworth, Yeats gives less prominence to childhood, and his world soul manifests in the human realm. It has cultural rather than natural roots. He thought it was the intellectual passion of a lifetime to develop them into a mature tree.

I don't have the space or the expertise to discuss all the facets of Yeats' evolving ideas on these issues. I am easily overwhelmed by his discussions of gyres and moon phases, and impatient with the technicalities of *A Vision*. I'm happy to imagine, falsely or otherwise, that the automatic writing and the experiments in conversing with spirits can be interpreted as metaphors for Yeats' thirst to connect with a world bigger than 'the frogspawn of a blind man's ditch', as he describes daily life in 'A Dialogue of Self and Soul'.

In his essay 'The Philosophy of Shelley's Poetry' from 1900, Yeats speaks of a Great Memory — a term that fittingly draws the distinction I have been trying to make with Wordsworth:

> Anyone who has any experience of any mystical state of the soul knows how there float up in the mind profound symbols . . . Nor I think has anyone . . . failed to find some day, in some old book or on some old monument, a strange or intricate image that had floated up before him, and to grow perhaps dizzy with the sudden conviction that our little memories are but a part of

some Great Memory that renews the world and men's thoughts age after age, and that our thoughts are not, as we suppose, the deep, but a little foam upon the deep.

This is a world of human archetypes, but there are elements in common with Wordsworth. The imagery of the sea, to start — a vast and mysterious realm. But equally the role of literature and art — some old book or monument — in keeping us in touch with this dimension, is common to both poets.

It is a commonplace to say we turn to the poems and stories of the past in search of wisdom — lessons to learn in order to avoid repeating past mistakes. But don't we also turn to old books and monuments to feel part of something bigger than the ditch of our own age? To experience that moment of awe when we glimpse ourselves as foam on a larger sea? This turning back should not be dismissed as nostalgia. That heritage we seek is the very manna of our soul, keeping us in touch with things bigger than ourselves and placing the realities of daily life into a vast context.

In *Per Amica Silentia Lunae,* Yeats describes how the poet and artist 'select our images from past times, we turn from our own age and try to feel Chaucer nearer than the daily paper'. We do this in order to connect with that Great Memory. By 1917, when *Per Amica* was published, that Great Memory has been linked to the idea of the antiself — the struggle to break out of the momentary aim by 'turning from the mirror to meditate upon a mask'. In the section of *Per Amica* called 'Anima Mundi' Yeats says:

I have always sought to bring my mind close to the mind of Indian and Japanese poets, old women in Connaught, mediums in Soho, lay brothers whom I imagine dreaming in some medieval monastery the dreams of their village, learned authors who refer all to antiquity; to immerse it in the great mind. . .

In reading authors of the past, and in wandering through museums, it seems to me we delight not only in the beauty or wisdom of masterpieces, but in our own ability to commune with them — to immerse ourselves in a general mind, to share thoughts, experiences, emotions, symbols with someone who lived 200 or 2000 years ago. I see our cultural heritage as a manifestation of Yeats' *anima mundi* or world soul, the mother from which we leaven the bread of our own lives. I marvel at the fact my tongue can quicken with the very words once used by Shakespeare and his contemporaries. Language is the great stream that flows through time and brings in its current the souls of the past who can appear to us in fleeting metempsychoses. We have the choice either to ignore this stream and continue to stare into the mirror, or to follow it out and swim in a vast and fathomless sea.

In Yeats' late poem 'Long-Legged Fly' I like to imagine the mysterious fly of the title is an image of the mind that is open to this heritage, and thus the mind that is fully human. It is the artistic mind that quests to create its artifice of eternity, and thereby allow civilization not to sink:

That civilization may not sink,
Its great battle lost,
Quiet the dog, tether the pony
To a distant post;
Our master Caesar is in the tent
Where the maps are spread,
His eyes fixed upon nothing,
A hand under his head.

Like a long-legged fly upon the stream
His mind moves upon silence.

Our great battle is against time, death, the muteness of life. We fight in order to perpetuate not our own idiosyncratic lives, but rather that legacy Yeats calls civilization here. Caesar in this first stanza, and then Michelangelo and Helen in the second and third stanzas of the poem, stand as three canonical examples of that civilization and its legacy. Thus the artist's mind moves upon silence, lifting itself up from the stream to walk. Is the stream in this poem an image of time or of civilization? The use of 'sink' in the first line would seem to suggest it is the passage of time. But I like to think Yeats would have been open to Dante's river of knowledge. In either case, what the poet creates is somehow miraculous, as miraculous as the insignificant insect who, in walking on water, imitates Jesus and defies both gravity and death.

The Australian poet Rosemary Dobson (1920–2012) came to articulate these ideas in a phrase: 'the continuance of poetry'. This was the title of a series of poems she wrote in memory of her contemporary David Campbell, and she took up the idea in an article published in *Island* Magazine in 1989 called 'Over my Shoulder'. There she writes: 'to be a poet is to put oneself in line in a long tradition'. She quotes one of her earlier poems, 'Still Life', which describes how that continuance manifests for her in the tradition of European painting. Here are the final two stanzas of the poem, which describes a still-life scene:

Whose was the hand that held the brush?
And who the guest who came to break
The loaf which I, three hundred years

Belated, still reach out to take?

I, who now pour the wine and tilt
The glass, would wish that well you fare,
Good sir, who set out food and drink
That all who see might take and share.

'Still Life' was from Dobson's second collection *The Ship of Ice* (1948). The banquet described here, in both painting and poem, recalls the Christian communion. It also recalls Auden, who wrote, 'one of the greatest blessings conferred on our lives by the Arts is that they are our chief means of breaking bread with the dead, and I think that, without communication with the dead, a fully human life is not possible'. The furnished table, like the river, is an image of plenty and nourishment of which we all partake.

These ideas reached poetic fruition in Dobson's third and fourth collections, to my mind her best, *Child With a Cockatoo* (1955) and *Cock Crow* (1965). One manifestation are the poems in *Child with a Cockatoo* that address figures in paintings, or are written in the voice of those figures. Take for example 'The Martyrdom of Saint Sebastian', quoted whole:

My scarlet coat lies on the ground,
You note the texture of the fur,
What miracles of art, you say,
Those Flemish painters could command,
Each brush-stroke like a single hair.

How the eye focuses upon
The archer stiffly draped in black
Cutting the foreground to the right —
Masterly, that foreshortened arm,

Skilful, the modelling of the neck.

How colour, line, and form combine
To give the painting depth and space!
Beyond the stream, beyond the hill,
The village — each receding plane
Leads to the sky the travelling glance.

And in the sky the angels throng
Like glittering birds upon a tree —
Marvellous, you say, the mind that takes
A fantasy upon the wing
And out of prose makes poetry.

I am Sebastian. While you praise
I suffer and my lips are dumb,
The arrows pierce me through and through,
Yet you admire with abstract phrase
The torment of my martyrdom.

What comes across is a love of these paintings which can still
speak to us and quicken our lives. The painter has captured each
brushstroke like a single hair. But the vision doesn't pin down
reality. It transforms it — turns prose to poetry, the mundane to
the magical. So when Sebastian says 'my lips are dumb', he lies,
and when he accuses the viewer's abstract phrase, it is undercut
by that transformative simile in the penultimate stanza, 'And in
the sky the angels throng / Like glittering birds upon a tree'. And
thus Sebastian continues to ask questions of us. He is an embodiment of the continuance of this heritage, this larger artwork that
contains both painting and poem. In 'Country Morning' it is the
poet with her 'curious, wilful eye', her 'inward eye', who casts the

spell to transform daily reality by contrasting it or blending it with that eternal world of art:

> The farmer's wife began her day
> With yawns and sighs and sleepy cries
> And though I knew she went to milk
> My inward eye saw otherwise.
> Oh strange — the rattle of the pail
> Was Phoebus shaking out his mail
> Who puts such glittering armour on.

In another poem, 'The Two Countries', that dichotomy between the quotidian reality of the present moment and the world of art take on geographically distinct characteristics. The world of art is associated with dream, it is 'the lost landscape of delight, / Its thickets, streams, and nightingales'. None of these, of course, are characteristic of the Australian landscape. Indeed the landscapes she evokes are often those found in the backgrounds of the paintings of the European Renaissance. I wonder whether part of the lack of interest in Dobson's early and middle period is an implicit criticism of this un-Australian focus. Her vision is decidedly Eurocentric. It asserts its independence from the cultural limitations of the Australia of her day, and also from British colonialism. But perhaps a political reading like this is overstating things. I suspect what's really going on is an attempt to reconnect with that *anima mundi* which has been the focus of this essay. Take for example 'The Cry':

> All day I walk in other worlds
> That intersect and meet in mine
> And yet one part of me I keep
> In silence waiting for a sign.

I am the innocent, the fool
Who listens for a far-off tune
Or feels the breath of evening stir
While it is yet the middle noon.

All day with diligence I go
That, pausing at a starry time
Or very early, I may catch
The brushing of celestial rhyme

As though some marvellous poetry
Were making in the air above
Where minds of poets meet and merge
Into a single cry of love.

What do these European landscapes have that ours do not have?
They have been transformed by the visions of artists over centuries, until they are layered with meanings like a rich fertile
soil from which new plants may grow. They are infused with
that Great Memory, that sphere 'where minds of poets meet and
merge'. It is the lifeblood of poetry and cannot be summoned
from nothing. It takes time for that accretion of human humus
to build up. It takes generations of leaf litter.

In the poem 'Child with a Cockatoo', Dobson describes a
portrait by S. Verelst of Anne, daughter of the Earl of Bedford,
in which an Australian cockatoo appears, well before Australia
was 'discovered' by Dampier or 'claimed' by Cook, when it was
still Terra Australis, an 'unimagined land'. Dobson's cockatoo is
described as 'That sulphur-crested bird with great white wings,
/ The wise, harsh bird — as old and wise as Time', and yet for
its European audiences it was 'a sign unread', 'a disregarded prologue to an age'. That is, it came from a world that had not yet

entered the maps of Europe, a world whose connections to the anima mundi were invisible to Europeans.

The various Aboriginal cultures had, of course, developed over millennia their own rich rivers flowing into that eternal sea. Few non-indigenous Australians have had the cultural knowledge to navigate them. Strehlow remains the great exception, but his *Songs of Central Australia* was not published until 1970. Furthermore, what Strehlow showed so admirably was the complexity of Arrernte traditions. Not only was the wealth of those cultures of a monumental scale, but song was shown to be intrinsically linked to dance and ritual, and to religion and identity. Its modes of expression and communication were shown to be radically different to Western art. As a result, attempts to engage with those songs from the outside easily appear tokenistic, an arrogation of the other rather than a borrowing in artistic homage.

Murray comes close to homage, bringing the two rivers into proximity, when, in his essay 'The Human-Hair Thread', he describes war memorials as 'stones of increase . . . they are, as it were, sacred sites from which a spirit, if not the spirits of the dead soldiers themselves, can be reborn, and the names incised on them are a sort of tjuringa of a past world'. The same impulse animates the poem 'The Returnees' from *Ethnic Radio*, where Murray catologues examples of an *anima-mundi*-like bass note to life:

. . . we
were conscious of a lifelong sound

on everything, that low fly-humming
melismatic untedious endless
note that a drone-pipe-plus-chants or

(shielding our eyes, rocking the river)

a ballad — some ballads — catch, the one
some paintings and many yarners summon
the ground-note here of unsnubbing art

cicadas were in it, and that Gothic
towering of crystals in the trees
Jock Neilson cutting a distant log

Not many Australian poets, however, have felt able to share
in Murray's confidence when he writes of artistic borrowing
from Aboriginal cultures that it is 'quite unlike the processes of
finance from which the metaphor is drawn: it leaves the lender
no poorer, and draws attention to his riches, which can only be
depleted by neglect and his loss of confidence in them'. Many
feel a persistant shyness. We are all too aware that such riches
have been depleted as a result of the wilful actions of those we
identify as our forebears.

That endless ground-note Murray celebrates in the poem
above seems to be located squarely in a rural Australia. There are
a series of light poems in *Cock Crow* in which Dobson reimagines
classical stories in an Australian setting. 'The Rape of Europa' is
among the best of them. Here is the first of six stanzas:

Beautiful Europa, while the billy boils
Underneath the she-oaks, underneath the willows,
Underneath the sky like a bent bow of silver,
Like the arms of a god embracing a mortal —
Beautiful Europa has set out a picnic.

To my mind the Australian setting doesn't ring true here. The
muse who stimulated Dobson's best work wasn't drinking at an

Australian rockpool, but the fountain of Parnassus. We already had Paterson with his swagman camped at the billabong, and his stranger throwing the stone across the Darling river at Walgett town in that wonderful poem 'Been There Before'. We already had the sea in Slessor's 'Five Bells' and Webb's 'For my Grandfather'. But Dobson was nourished by other waters, or by trees with deeper roots, taproots that take millenia to grow. Something as old as Knossos, that Bronze age city in Crete. Here are the opening two stanzas of the poem of that title:

> Impossible to build the palace again over our heads,
> The painted roof-beams, the cisterns, the great granary,
> Impossible to think of people living simply,
> Going about their errands in the sunshine,
> The king receiving supplicants in the throne-room.
>
> In the empty courtyard by the fallen columns
> It is possible, nevertheless, to feel continuance.
> A cock crows in the valley, noonday
> Exhales resin, sunlight settles
> almost like thin golden beaten petals, . . .

This is from the period following *Cock Crow* in which she begins to be formally freer, and newly under the influence of Eastern European writers such as Miłosz. The interest in the continuance of a deeper past remains.

In 'The Human-Hair Thread' Murray talks of two hundred years being long enough for a vernacular culture to establish itself. 'Forty thousand years', he says, 'are not very different from a few hundred, if your culture has not, through genealogy, developed a sense of the progression of time and thus made history possible.' But as I have tried to describe in this essay, it's not a question of progress. Two hundred years is time enough for a river red gum to reach a respectable size, but it needs to have been seeded on the floodplains of a much older river if it is to flourish. That river water is equally timeless in Aboriginal cultures and in Europe. It is the *anima mundi* that feeds the tree, not the billy water of a wandering swagman. Murray's poems know this — they contain some of the best examples in Australia of a poetry in touch with what is 'always there'. I suspect, however, that the opposition Murray developed between derivative high culture and distinctive vernacular culture has prejudiced us against such expressions of that 'ground-note' which take their bearings from a classical heritage.

I find in Rosemary Dobson one of our best celebrations of this rich continuance of poetry. I love the way she gives expression to the miracle that makes such continuance possible. Knossos, like the Roman Forum, is full of the signs of ruin, and yet it defies time to nourish our imagination still. As Dobson says at the end of the poem 'Of Poetry', it is marvellous:

The boy who lay asleep
Between the rows of vines
Heard the god speak in dream.

'Then Aischylos awoke
And wrote as he was bid.'
So said Pausanias.

I have walked out of town.
Soon I'll lie down and sleep
Between the rows of vines

Planted like lines of verse,
Like sweet, syllabic lines
In ordered fall and rise,

Laden with fruit to make
Libations of dark wine
For Dionysos.

And he, the god, perhaps
Will speak to me in dream
As once to Aischylos.

Marvellous! Marvellous!

## Works Cited

W. H. Auden, *Prose Volume VI 1969–1973*, ed. Edward Mendelson, Princeton University Press, 2015.

Dante, *Opere minori, tomo II, De Monarchia*, ed. Pier Vincenzo Mengaldo and Bruno Nardi, Riccardo Ricciardi Editore, 1979.

Rosemary Dobson, 'Over my Shoulder', *Island Magazine*, 1989.

Rosemary Dobson, *Collected*, University of Queensland Press, 2012.

Robert Gray, *Cumulus. Collected Poems*, John Leonard Press, 2012.

John Milton, *The Poetical Works of John Milton*, ed. Helen Darbishire, Oxford University Press, 1958.

Les Murray, 'The Human-Hair Thread', in *Persistence in Folly*, Sirius Books, 1984.

Les Murray, *Collected Poems*, Angus and Robertson, 1988.

T. G. H. Strehlow, *Songs of Central Australia*, Angus and Robertson, 1971.

Lisa Sullivan, 'In detail: Christine O'Loughlin Cultural Rubble', The Ian Potter Museum of Art, 2002.

William Wordsworth, *Selected Prose*, Penguin, 1988.

W. B. Yeats, *The Collected Poems of W. B. Yeats*, revised second edition, ed. Richard J. Finneran, Scribner, 1989.

W. B. Yeats, *Essays and Introductions*, MacMillan, 1961.

W. B. Yeats, *Later Essays*, ed. William H. O'Donnell, Scribner, 1994.

# Acknowledgements

These pieces were written between 2011 and 2018. In most cases they began as talks and essays to mark particular occasions, or as reviews. While they have been reworked, they also preserve some traits of the original circumstances that brought them into being. I would like to thank the editors of publications where earlier versions first appeared, in particular *The Weekend Australian* and *The Sydney Review of Books*. 'Living Walls of Jet' was given as a talk at the Mildura Writers Festival; 'As if We Were God's Spies' was presented at a symposium on poetry and translation in Melbourne organised by Aalitra; and 'Squaring the Circle' was first a talk given at Swinburne University.

www.ingramcontent.com/pod-product-compliance
Lightning Source LLC
Chambersburg PA
CBHW030830090426
42737CB00009B/952